"I love this book! It's full of . . . evangelism but, far from just f . . . heart with passion. Richard not . . . reminds us of why and how we should share our faith but also inspires us to get on with it."

VAUGHAN ROBERTS, *Rector of St Ebbe's Church, Oxford,*
and Director of the Proclamation Trust

"This is the most readable and accessible commentary on the book of Jonah. The story of the prophet is filled with surprising twists and turns—and loads of lessons for us today. Richard is a trustworthy and insightful guide to the readers of this book. It will be a boon to preachers and listeners alike."

TIMOTHY KELLER, *Pastor Emeritus,*
Redeemer Presbyterian Church, New York City

"Some expositions of Jonah almost entirely miss God's evangelistic compassion—infinitely stronger than that of the prophet Jonah. Not so this popular exposition, written with verve and panache by Richard Coekin. Coekin thinks through what it means to lose our reluctance to be evangelists. Above all, he reminds us of what Jonah rediscovered: 'Salvation comes from the LORD'!"

D.A. CARSON, *Research Professor of New Testament at Trinity*
Evangelical Divinity School, and President of The Gospel Coalition

"This gripping book is packed with compelling reasons and practical encouragement to spread the good news of Jesus Christ. It both inspires and equips the 'reluctant evangelist'."

WILLIAM TAYLOR, *Rector of St Helen's Bishopsgate, London*

"I have thoroughly enjoyed the deft exegetical touch displayed in 'The Reluctant Evangelist'. It's accurate and light, faithful and pertinent. I thoroughly recommend it!"

STEVE TIMMIS, *CEO, Acts 29*

"As Christians we know that we ought to be passionately committed to evangelism, but many of us are reluctant to share the good news about Jesus with others. Richard Coekin rightly identifies that our main problem is a lack of motivation. Rather than inducing unproductive and discouraging guilt, in this compelling short book he expounds the well-known story of Jonah, and urges us to see the compassionate character and sovereign saving purposes of God. Written with clarity and directness, and packed with personal testimonies and engaging illustrations, no one who reads this book will fail to be inspired, encouraged and empowered to overcome their reluctance in personal evangelism. Many churches would be greatly blessed if the whole congregation were to read the book together, and it is an ideal resource for discussion in small groups, perhaps taking a chapter each week for reflection and prayer."

JOHN STEVENS, *National Director,*
Fellowship of Independent Evangelical Churches (FIEC)

RICHARD COEKIN

The Reluctant Evangelist

MOVING FROM *CAN'T* AND *DON'T*
TO *CAN* AND *DO*

thegoodbook
COMPANY

For my dad, John, with love and everlasting gratitude
because, like Caleb, you
"followed the LORD my God wholeheartedly"
and encouraged your family to do the same
Joshua 14 v 8

The Reluctant Evangelist: *Moving from can't and don't to can and do*
© Richard Coekin/The Good Book Company, 2018.

Published by
The Good Book Company
Tel (UK): 0333 123 0880
International: +44 (0) 208 942 0880
Email: info@thegoodbook.co.uk

Websites:
UK: www.thegoodbook.co.uk
North America: www.thegoodbook.com
Australia: www.thegoodbook.com.au
New Zealand: www.thegoodbook.co.nz

ISBN: 9781784983413 | Printed in the UK

Design by Ben Woodcraft

CONTENTS

PREFACE

This is a book for *reluctant evangelists*. I mean it's for Christians who generally find it difficult to engage in evangelistic conversations, daunting to consider joining a church plant, and utterly terrifying to engage in cross-cultural mission.

Indeed, this is a book by someone who has been a reluctant evangelist. Some years ago, before I was a pastor and church-planter, I managed to invite a friend I'd known at university called Rachel to come to a guest service at my church in London. When I phoned to remind her to come, her flatmate Sarah explained that Rachel had gone away for the weekend with friends. "Why, what were you inviting her to?" she asked. "Oh, nothing much," I replied, feeling embarrassed. "No really," she insisted. "Where were you going?" "Oh, just church—don't worry about it," I mumbled. "Oh great—can I come instead?" said Sarah brightly.

So she came to church that Sunday, and when the evangelist finished preaching, he asked if those who wanted to become Christians would come to the front of the congregation to be prayed for. To my complete shock, Sarah stood up and walked down to the front to become a Christian! My pathetic evangelistic reluctance was brutally exposed that night.

For some of us, our reluctance is *temperamental*—perhaps we're a little shy, reserved or introverted in character, and evangelism feels frightening.

For others of us, our reluctance is *cultural*—we've been raised to keep to ourselves, and evangelism seems rude.

For many of us, our reluctance is *theological*—we're just not sure if God wants all Christians to engage in mission, especially if we lack the gifts or "calling" in evangelism that others seem to have.

For most of us, our reluctance is *motivational*—we have so many responsibilities and problems to face that we're not persuaded that evangelism should really be an urgent priority for us right now.

But evangelism is not *optional* for Christians. When our Lord Jesus first called his disciples he said, "Come, follow me, and I will send you out to fish for people"; later he warned them, "If anyone is ashamed of me and my words in this adulterous and sinful generation, the Son of Man will be ashamed of them when he comes in his Father's glory"; and when he left them he commanded, "Go and make disciples of all nations" (Matthew 4 v 19; Mark 8 v 38; Matthew 28 v 19). So his apostle Peter insists, "Always be prepared to give an answer to everyone who asks you to give the reason for the hope that you have" (1 Peter 3 v 15).

Thankfully, our reluctance is *treatable*—we really don't have to find evangelism so hard or frightening. For, as we shall see, Almighty God is a compassionate Evangelist, and his Spirit can transform us by his word to share his passion for mission. He really can teach us to find personal evangelism, church-planting and cross-cultural mission exciting—indeed the fulfilling purpose of our lives.

So *The Reluctant Evangelist* aims to help you conquer your reluctance—to follow Jesus unashamedly in making disciples for him, ready to explain your hope in language your family, friends and colleagues can understand.

We will explore God's basic mission principles as they are beautifully clarified in the gripping memoirs of the prophet Jonah, read in the light of Christ and the rest of the Bible. In our church and church-planting movement in London, we've discovered that all the foundational principles we've needed are to be found here; because Jonah is not just a children's bedtime story about a big fish (the whale is a "red herring" anyway!). Rather, Jonah is a serious mission-training manual from our God, the compassionate Evangelist, who has not only delayed the end of the world but sent his beloved Son to die on a cross, in order to evangelise the nations.

As we shall discover, effective evangelism begins with understanding the character and purposes of the living and loving God revealed in Jonah and fulfilled in Christ. It's only when we learn to *trust* his awesome *power* (chapter 1), *experience* his sovereign *grace* (chapter 2), *fear* his coming *judgment* (chapter 3) and *share* his gut-wrenching *compassion* (chapter 4)—as this is perfectly revealed in Jesus, the divine Evangelist—that our hearts will sing with the melodic line of Jonah, "Salvation comes from the LORD" (Jonah 2 v 9). And when his Holy Spirit fills our hearts with *his* love, our lives will start to bubble up with the evangelistic enterprise that our friends, colleagues, communities and cities so desperately need.

The Reluctant Evangelist is not trying to sell you yet another "silver bullet" outreach strategy because I don't think that is what most of us need (though I hope some of the missional ideas will be helpful). Instead, I pray that this book will help you access the fundamental and thrilling evangelistic principles of Jonah, to understand how God is reaching unbelievers everywhere today.

For if God can use someone as reluctant and selfish as Jonah to accomplish the greatest urban revival in Bible history (when the whole pagan city of Nineveh turned to the LORD), he can use us too.

OUR LORD
CAN SAVE ANYONE

Read the whole of Jonah quickly to get the story

Think for a moment about the city or town where you live. Do you think anyone who lives there is beyond salvation through faith in Christ Jesus? Do you think some people are so immoral or evil that God doesn't want to save them? Or that some people are so indoctrinated by Islam or atheism that they cannot be reached by our Lord? Or has someone you care about proved so apathetic, resistant or hostile to the gospel that you have nearly given up hope of them ever becoming a Christian?

Well, Almighty God once dramatically demonstrated that he can save anyone by saving *a whole city* of violent, idolatrous pagans in one go! The Old Testament book of Jonah describes how our Lord once brought the entire 8th-century-BC city of Nineveh to salvation—through a very reluctant evangelist proclaiming his gospel. Now, when Christians think about the towns and cities where we live today, and about the unbelievers we care most about, we will want to know more about how that happened.

For example, London, where I have lived with my family for the last twenty-three years, is certainly an exciting, cosmopolitan city with great influence in our nation and the world. Ever since the 2012 Olympics, the Mori Global Power City Index has consistently ranked London as "Number 1 City in the World", leaving New York, Tokyo and Paris trailing in its wake. It's a political, economic and cultural powerhouse. And it is home to 8.8 million people from a rich diversity of backgrounds. For the nations have come to London for education, business and a better life. Less than half of its population are now white British: 600,000 people state their ethnicity as Indian, 400,000 are French, there are 230,000 each from Pakistan and Bangladesh, indeterminate hundreds of thousands from Poland, Romania and Bulgaria, and 80,000 Somalis. And the city is constantly churning with a net annual growth of about 100,000. London is a multicultural global city and I love it.

But this city is also an emerging spiritual catastrophe. When the 2011 National Census asked, "What religion are you?", 48% of Londoners replied "Christian". However, the Times YouGov survey of 2015 revealed that only 55% of them believe in God. The London City Mission census of 2012 revealed that only 9% of Londoners are attending church on Sunday—and only 5.4% are attending evangelical churches. (UK church 2010-2020 Statistics, Peter Brierley, Brierley consultancy, ADBC publishing 2014, page 61, section 12.1)

I can only conclude from these figures that more than 90% of Londoners would claim no saving faith in Christ and so are hurtling towards eternal misery. And if your city or town is currently in better spiritual shape, there is little cause for complacency, because multiple forces of globalisation threaten to drag many population centres of the world in the same spiritual direction as London.

As I was studying my Bible on a train recently, a British student sitting opposite me observed, "That's a fat book!" "It's a Bible," I replied, and then asked, "Have you read about Jesus in it?" This educated young woman knew *nothing* about the Bible or about Jesus Christ, because a secular atheistic intelligentsia have been aggressively emptying our media, schools and public life of gospel-teaching in the name of "cultural tolerance", for the major world religions are here. According to the 2011 Census there are more than a million Muslims, (more than 12% of Londoners, including the current mayor, Sadiq Khan); more than 450,000 Hindus (5% of Londoners), and numerous Sikhs, Buddhists and Jews. An older generation of Londoners may visit church at Christmas and want their grandchildren "christened"; but the prevailing ideology of younger generations, vigorously promoted by our popular media across most ethnic and socioeconomic boundaries, is an individualistic, libertine hedonism— haunted by a little superstitious mysticism.

To generalise, our city is no longer a lapsed Christian city in need of revival (such as God brought wonderfully in the 18th century) but a pagan pre-Christian city that needs to be re-evangelised, much like the 8th-century-BC Nineveh of Jonah's day. I suspect this is increasingly true of most Westernised cities. In London we live in a mission-field—in a commonwealth of communities without God, without hope and desperately in need of the gospel of Christ.

Indeed, in our Co-Mission church-planting movement, we have often observed the sobering parallels between cities like London and the tragic sinking of the ocean liner *Titanic* when it hit an iceberg in 1912 and 1500 passengers died. The appalling loss of life was hugely increased by *four* factors:

a. The desperate shortage of lifeboats—as we need hundreds more gospel-teaching churches for the different communities of our cities.

b. A woeful lack of lifeboat training for the crew—as we need better training in personal evangelism, church-planting and cross-cultural mission.

c. A wicked neglect of poorer passengers, who were locked in the lower decks while the rich boarded the life-boats—as we need more churches for the poorer districts of our cities. *But most serious of all...*

d. A shocking lack of compassion among the passengers in the half-empty lifeboats hovering around the mass of desperate people drowning in the icy waters, unwilling to go back for fear of being overwhelmed. They waited until the screaming stopped and then returned to collect the bodies—as too many of our half-empty churches are neglecting the desperate spiritual need of their communities who are drowning in their sin. Too many churches are effectively hiding until the screaming has stopped for fear of being swamped by the need or hostility out there, until it's time to emerge and offer a funeral service to bury the dead. We have got to do better than that—haven't we?

But where will we find the sustaining motivation, the sensible training, the appropriate sense of responsibility and, above all, the sacrificial compassion for evangelism, church-planting and cross-cultural mission? I'm convinced that these treasures are to be found in this extraordinary Old Testament book of Jonah.

Jonah gives us the essential foundations we need

We have to understand God's missional strategy revealed in the Bible before we can clarify an effective missional strategy for our towns and cities, friends and family. And that's what Jonah gives us—God's basic evangelistic strategy for saving people in every community of every city in every generation. Jonah gives us the *foundational evangelistic theology* that is our primary need.

Please don't mishear me—I'm all for creative missional strategies and for contextualising our ministries (without contextualising our gospel). In other contexts, I try to champion the value of excellent training in apologetics, evangelistic exposition, connective media and biblical counselling (helping us see the connections between the gospel and personal needs as Jesus did in his evangelistic conversations). But across our Co-Mission churches, we are discovering that the principles revealed when God evangelised Nineveh in the 8th-century BC, using a reluctant evangelist called Jonah, are still the effective first principles for evangelising cities like London today.

So let me introduce you briefly to the amazing memoirs of the prophet Jonah.

Jonah is beautifully crafted

Indeed, Jonah is a literary masterpiece. Secular scholars get a bit *seasick* studying it—they find the big fish *hard to swallow*. But Jonah isn't primarily about "Jonah and the whale". It's about the LORD... and a reluctant evangelist. Unlike the writings of some other Minor Prophets who emphasize that the LORD is our judge, Jonah explains that our LORD is deeply reluctant to judge because he is also merciful. Indeed, God was determined to train the rebellious prophet Jonah to preach his gospel, and through him God called the godless city of Nineveh to turn to him. And in enabling Jonah to record his training, the Lord was also training his people, then and now. The apostle Paul reminds us that everything written here was written for our encouragement (Romans 15 v 4)—and this tale is wonderfully encouraging for anyone who wants to learn how to be evangelistic.

The book has a carefully crafted structure to emphasise its primary themes. It has:

- a central declaration
- two parallel halves
- four chapters
- a challenging conclusion
- a glorious fulfilment
- a lasting imperative

Jonah has a marvellous **central declaration** in Jonah 2 v 9: "Salvation comes from the LORD". This truth is illustrated by the salvation of pagan sailors from a storm, the salvation of the disobedient prophet from drowning, and the salvation of the city of Nineveh from destruction. The central message of the book is that *God himself is an evangelistic Saviour.*

So the living Lord we commend to others is also a loving Saviour; and when we try to evangelise our communities, colleagues and friends, we are engaged in our Lord's business: his highest priority for his world, the activity he most delights to find in his children and his churches. Biblical evangelism is not the poor cousin of Bible exposition, for the ruffians who can't be scholars. Rather, if "salvation comes from the LORD", then biblical exposition serves to equip God's people for lives of biblical evangelism.

Jonah has **two parallel halves** (chapters 1 – 2 and chapters 3 – 4). Each begins with God's command, followed by his judgment and then by his mercy. The first half in chapters 1 – 2, recounts the salvation of Jonah, and its central declaration is in 1 v 9: "I am a Hebrew and I worship the LORD, the God of heaven, who made the sea and the dry land". The second half in chapters 3 – 4 recounts the salvation of Nineveh, and its central declaration is in 4 v 2: "I knew that you are a gracious and compassionate God, slow to anger and abounding in love".

Like us, Jonah needed to learn from both halves of this book: the Lord who is our Creator is also the Lord who is our Saviour. This encourages us to pray for help in evangelism to our Lord, who is both the awesomely powerful Creator (to give us strength and courage) and the gracious compassionate Saviour (to give us his patience and love). And it's clear that God gave Jonah his own dramatic personal experience of God's mercy in chapters 1 – 2 to prepare him for Nineveh receiving mercy in chapters 3 – 4, just as our personal experience of mercy in Christ should motivate us to help others find his mercy too. We are not to live on the beach at the end of chapter 2, rejoicing in our own salvation until we die.

We need to recognise that our experience of God's mercy is only half of our story too. We have experienced God's mercy *for the purpose* of helping others experience his mercy; like Jonah, we must embark upon the second half of our lives. After all, *evangelism is why God has delayed the end of the world and why Christians are still here and not in heaven*—"he is patient with you, not wanting anyone to perish, but everyone to come to repentance" (2 Peter 3 v 9).

Jonah has **four chapters**: each emphasising one missional aspect of the LORD's breathtaking *character*—and each is combined with one of his mind-blowing *attributes*:

- Chapter 1: His **holiness** is combined with his **omnipotence** (unlimited power).
- Chapter 2: His **grace** is combined with his **omnipresence** (unrestricted involvement).
- Chapter 3: His **wrath** is combined with his **relenting** (promised mercy).
- Chapter 4: His **compassion** is combined with his **providence** (constant care).

These are *beautiful* personal virtues combined with *stunning* attributes of power. Our Lord is indeed both captivating and amazing! And as we admire these magnificent qualities, theologians remind us that God is "simple" or "maximally alive", meaning he is all his qualities all the time. For he is one personal God, who acts differently in different situations but without losing any of his perfections, like a fire that may bring welcome warmth or helpful light or terrifying devastation in different contexts, while always remaining fire. So we cannot select one characteristic of our Lord and reject another (for example, delighting in his mercy but ignoring his wrath), for he is always fully himself. While the chapters focus upon different aspects of God's character and power, as a prism separates out the different elements of light, we must remember that he is always maximally alive in all of them, so we will humble ourselves before this Lord who is both beautiful and terrifying at the same time.

And in this revelation of his marvellous qualities, he intends to bring us intense enjoyment: for, as the great 17th-century Westminster Shorter Catechism famously reads, *"Man's chief end is to glorify God, and to enjoy him for ever"*. In his important book, *Desiring God*, John Piper explains that this means that we "glorify God **by** enjoying him". Piper rightly concludes, *"God is most glorified in us when we are most satisfied in him"*. So we're going to thoroughly enjoy God as we study Jonah; and as we marvel and delight in him, we will want to glorify him by telling others about him. Indeed, do stop to pray as you read through this book—for if we don't want to praise God to his face, we will never want to praise him to other people.

Allow me to illustrate: last year, my wife and I watched a live performance by the supergroup *Coldplay* at the packed Principality Stadium in Cardiff. The lead singer, Chris Martin, was amazing—and singing along to such iconic anthems as "Paradise", "Clocks" and "Fix You" was so much fun. I couldn't stop talking about *Coldplay* for weeks! So it is with God. When we are amazed and delighted by God, we won't struggle to commend him to others. When we can celebrate with the psalmist, "The LORD has done great things for us, and we are filled with joy" (Psalm 126 v 3), we can willingly respond to the psalmist's call to evangelise the world: "Declare his glory among the nations, his marvellous deeds among all peoples" (Psalm 96 v 3).

In another important book, *Let the Nations be glad*, Piper observes:

> *"Worship, therefore, is the fuel and goal of missions. It's the goal of missions because in missions we simply aim to bring the nations into the white-hot enjoyment of God's glory. The goal of missions is the gladness of the peoples in the greatness of God ... [but] where passion for God is weak, zeal for missions will be weak."*
>
> *(Let the Nations be Glad, pages 35-36)*

So do marvel at our Lord as we study this extraordinary revival; for enjoying the greatness of God in Jonah is *fuel for our evangelism*. Our first need in personal evangelism, church-planting and cross-cultural mission must be a fresh delight in Christ, before it is strategic insight. The main reason most of us struggle to speak about Christ to friends and colleagues is not because we're struggling to understand our culture, but because we're not very excited about God. Jonah can fix that!

Jonah has a **challenging conclusion** in the Lord's question that echoes down the ages in the final words of the book: "Should I not have concern for [that] great city?" These words call us to both celebrate and share in God's compassionate concern for people from all nations, however foreign or evil they may seem to us.

Jonah has a **glorious fulfilment** in the greatest prophet, Jesus, who said, "A wicked and adulterous generation asks for a sign! But none will be given it except the sign of the prophet Jonah" (Matthew 12 v 39). As we shall see, Jesus was speaking of himself as being like Jonah, the resurrected preacher for our generation, who is the sign from God, the divine evangelist that our cities and friends will need. For behind the many Bible-writers there is one directing author, the Spirit of God, and behind the various covenantal periods there is one uniting history, the kingdom of God, and behind the various prophets, priests and kings there is one central hero, the Son of God. This requires us to interpret Jonah in relation to Jesus Christ: for the missional themes explored in Jonah all find their fulfilment in the divine Evangelist, Jesus.

And Jonah has a **lasting imperative**: for when the LORD twice commands Jonah in 1 v 2 and 3 v 2, "Go to the great city of Nineveh!" it is the authorial intention of the Holy Spirit that we hear Christ's command to his disciples in all generations (including us) in Matthew 28 v 19: "Go and make disciples of all nations". Jonah's memoirs recount the heartwarming tale of how the LORD saved a whole city of sinners, through and despite the disobedient reluctance and shocking selfishness of his messenger. God is showing us that his holy love is expressed in our world today primarily in recruiting ordinary, screwed-up people like us into his mission to save sinners. And if he used a reluctant evangelist like Jonah, he can use us too.

Holiness is evangelistic

Even in this brief introduction, it has become obvious that our holiness in this world must be evangelistic! Evangelism will cease when we get to heaven (though we'll always celebrate the gospel of Jesus, the slain Lamb of God—Revelation 5). But until we get to heaven, the primary purpose of *our lives* must be the same as *God's primary purpose in the world*, which is to glorify him through evangelism.

When the disciples saw Jesus risen from the dead, "they worshipped him" (Matthew 28 v 17) with a devotion due to God. Then Jesus commanded them to express their worship by making disciples, for being saved into a vertical life of worship leads to the horizontal activity of mission. They're not alternatives or competitors but partners; and so *the defining activity of a church is Bible-teaching that equips God's people for lives of worship expressed in evangelising the nations.*

So the first principle of Jonah is that **our Lord can save anyone and wants to save everyone**—for he is "God our Saviour, who wants all people to be saved and to come to a knowledge of the truth" (1 Timothy 2 v 3-4).

Personal evangelism, church-planting and cross-cultural mission are not optional minority sports for a few hardy zealots! Rather, true godliness is not just the absence of wickedness but the presence of compassionate commitment to evangelism. And we see this most vividly in Christ: for when he took flesh in Jesus, he came as the greatest evangelist, church-planter and cross-cultural missionary of all time. So let us pray that, through reading Jonah, we will become *a lot less like Jonah, and a lot more like Jesus.*

OUR LORD IS OFFENDED BY THE SIN OF ALL NATIONS

Read Jonah 1 v 1-2

Why do the nations need saving anyway? What is God's problem? Why can't he just forgive and forget what people do wrong? In fact, why do the nations need a Saviour at all?

Jonah 1 begins by demonstrating that God expresses his sovereignty over the nations in global evangelism. At first, it sounds as if God intends to send Jonah to Nineveh as his agent of condemnation, for he says to Jonah:

> *"Go to the great city of Nineveh ... because its wickedness has come up before me."* *(Jonah 1 v 2)*

But, as we shall see later (and as Jonah guessed from the beginning), Jonah's message of judgment was actually part of the gospel message through which the LORD always intended to bring salvation to Nineveh. The LORD who rules over all nations was offended by the wickedness of the people of

Nineveh, a city far away from Israel, so he sent Jonah to bring them to repentance so that they would experience his mercy. Indeed, it seems the LORD intended to remind all Israel to accept their calling to be a blessing from God to all nations. The same thing happened when Jesus was resurrected and announced his plan for his world. He began:

> *"All authority in heaven and on earth has been given to me.*
> ***Therefore**, go and make disciples of all nations."*
> *(Matthew 28 v 18-19)*

That is, Christ is expressing his sovereign lordship over all nations today primarily in evangelistic mission.

But why is God so offended by the sin of all nations, then and now, that they need saving from his wrath? And why does he go to such extreme lengths to get a reluctant evangelist like Jonah to Nineveh to proclaim his message? As with the Mediterranean Sea, we won't discover how exciting this is until we're swimming in it. So let's jump in.

In Jonah 1 v 1-2 we are introduced to the main characters described in the book of Jonah and, in particular, to the sovereignty of God.

The LORD

First, we meet *the LORD*, written in capitals to show that this was his awesome and ancient name "Yahweh", meaning "I am who I am" (or "I will be who I will be"). This is the personal name of God revealed to Moses from a burning bush (Exodus 3 v 14) so that we may know him. It asserts his absolute power, or "*omnipotence*"—his sovereign freedom to be and do whatever he chooses. (We rejoice to discover that he would use his freedom to keep his covenant promise to rescue his chosen people—*then* this was the people of Israel, enslaved in Pharaoh's Egypt, and *now* it is all whom he chooses to save through the gospel—sinners enslaved by the world, the flesh and the devil.)

This LORD clearly assumes that his prophet Jonah will understand the responsibility of his people toward all nations, for he has always redeemed people from slavery into his missional purposes: "Sing to the LORD, praise his name; proclaim his salvation day after day. Declare his glory among the nations, his marvellous deeds among all peoples" (Psalm 96 v 2-3). This was why Jesus was later so angry to discover the temple courts in Jerusalem being used for commercial business instead of welcoming people from all nations to approach God for salvation in prayer—quoting the promise of Isaiah 56: "My house will be called a house of prayer for all nations" (Mark 11 v 17). And he's entitled to be worshipped by every person in every community in every city, because Christ is already enthroned in heaven over all nations, cultures and communities. Evangelism is not arrogant or imperialistic—but a wonderful public information service, telling the world about the One who now rules all nations.

The phrase "the word of the LORD came" is repeated over a hundred times in the Old Testament—for God exercises his rule by his Spirit through his word. This is why the defining activity of every church should be gathering together to hear God's word. Churches are not think tanks for debating what to do but schools for training us to obey his commands—where God's Spirit equips us for God's work through God's word! Since God is sovereign over everyone, he's entitled to command Jonah, and us, where to go.

The LORD was sovereign over the prophet Jonah

Jonah was a prophet of God in the early 8th century BC, from Gath Hepher, near Nazareth. He was the son of an unremarkable man called Amittai. In 2 Kings 14 v 25 we discover that, despite Israel's constant rebellion, when the power of Assyria in the north became weak, God employed Jonah to announce his blessing upon Israel by extending Israel's borders to their former glory. Now the LORD sends Jonah, the same prophet who announced blessing to Israel, to bring blessing to the foreigners, the pagan Assyrians. This was just as the LORD had once promised to Abraham—that his descendants would bring blessing to all nations (Genesis 12 v 3)—a promise later identified as the gospel (Galatians 3 v 8).

One would think that Jonah would be glad of this opportunity to share the blessings of the knowledge of God with others. For example, it has been hugely encouraging to hear mission-hearted Christians in Kenya and Korea, having received the gospel from England and Wales respectively, speaking of their sense of obligation to send their missionaries back to our land, now that we are a spiritual desert and mission-field once more. I shall never forget coming to our church building to welcome a Korean mission conference, to find 400 Koreans on their knees, mostly in tears, all crying out aloud to the Lord at the same time, as is their custom.

"What are they praying about with such passion?" I asked my Korean colleague.

"They are praying for this country," he replied. That was humbling.

But like many in Israel then and among us now, Jonah didn't care for the people of Nineveh. He would prove to be selfish, spiteful, and even racist—lacking compassion for unbelievers of other nations. God had arranged for this prophet to be named "Jonah", which means "dove", a Hebrew idiom for silliness. For indeed, the LORD's discipline would expose him as a bit of a clown—and his experiences were, frankly, farcical: thrown overboard into the sea, swallowed by a fish, spewed onto a beach, and after a great revival, sitting outside Nineveh having a tantrum about a bush!

Sadly, Jonah is uncomfortably like us. As God's prophet, Jonah should have cheerfully obeyed his sovereign LORD. So also all Christians should be cheerfully obeying God's commission to make disciples of all nations. After all, since God poured out his Holy Spirit on the day of Pentecost, we have all received the Spirit to be his prophets, declaring the wonders of God in Jesus (Acts 2 v 11). But too often we won't. God has given Jonah to us as a mirror in which to see some ugly truths about ourselves.

The LORD was sovereign over the city of Nineveh

By ancient standards, Nineveh was a major city of 120,000 people, already a royal residence in the Assyrian empire. But the LORD's opinion of Nineveh is revealed in two significant words, "*great*" and "*wicked*".

First, Nineveh was "*great*"—not so much because it was important (Jonah 3 v 1) politically and commercially, but because, as God later observes, it was full of spiritually clueless people in need of the gospel for salvation (Jonah 4 v 11). That is primarily why cities must matter to us—not just because they shape national and global cultures (significant though that is) but because they are densely populated with precious people who are pouring like lemmings over the cliffs of death into an eternity of torment in the fiery caverns of hell.

So it's loving to seek the welfare of the city in every way—but *especially* with the gospel of Christ, which grants eternal welfare. In the perennial debates about the relative importance of social action and of evangelism, it is surely obvious that while we must seek the welfare of others in every way we can, we must above all seek the *eternal welfare* of unbelievers in proclaiming the gospel, so that they can be saved from the horrors of hell for the happiness of heaven. Because eternity is a very, very long time!

This is not to diminish the importance of social justice and compassion. The Bible celebrates our Creator's concern for our whole being, including our physical, social and spiritual needs; for example, "I am the LORD, who exercises kindness, justice and righteousness on earth, for in these I delight" (Jeremiah 9 v 24). The needy whom God cares about are repeatedly described in four categories: *orphans* (including children aborted or neglected), *widows* (including women abused and trafficked), *foreigners* (including asylum seekers at our borders and the homeless on our streets), and *the poor* (including many single parents, and elderly, disabled and long-term unemployed people struggling to make ends meet). And when this God took flesh in Jesus, his kindness towards those he came across who were sick or in need was legendary, not only in demonstrating his identity as the divine King and the nature of his coming kingdom, but in his gut-wrenching compassion for the crowds. He saw them as "harassed and helpless" (meaning stressed and burdened) because they were like sheep without a shepherd (that is, desperately in need of him). Christians should seek social justice and welfare, especially for the weak, wherever we can. This is not just for a manipulative ulterior motive of gaining a hearing for the gospel but because it is the loving thing to do; though godly compassion often does gain the respect of unbelievers and the opportunity to share our motivation in the gospel of Christ, "so that in every way [we] will make the teaching about God our Saviour attractive" (Titus 2 v 10). Our Lord's primary evangelistic strategy in his world has always been the godliness of his people.

But Jesus was also quite plain that **everyone's greatest need is for the gospel**. So when choices must be made with our time and resources, we must follow his example by making it our priority to invest in gospel ministry that will meet the primary need of the nations, for it is the gospel that brings eternal relief in the new creation. As Jesus said when the needs of the sick threatened to distract him from his evangelistic preaching, "Let us go somewhere else—to the nearby villages—so that I can preach there also. That is why I have come" (Mark 1 v 38). And when confronted with a paralysed man lowered through the roof of the house where he was preaching, he declared, "Your sins are forgiven" (Mark 2 v 5). This was not because the man's paralysis was caused by his sin (which is false theology and, if true, would have meant the man was healed immediately when he was forgiven) but because the greatest need of every human being, even a paralysed man with such obvious physical need, is to have their sins forgiven. After all, that man is now in paradise with Christ. Which miracle experienced in that unforgettable meeting with Jesus do you think he is now thanking God for most: his forgiveness or his healing? His forgiveness for sure.

Indeed, gospel ministry is also the most potent force for social transformation now, because Christ calls sinners to repent from damaging sin and empowers us with his Spirit so that marriages and communities can be gradually restored. So Nineveh, London, Beijing, New Delhi, Moscow, Lagos and our town or city may be "great" for many reasons—but primarily because they are home to so many precious people who need to hear God's gospel message explained in a language they can understand!

Why would the Lord want to save Nineveh?

Second, Nineveh was "*wicked*" (evil)—a broad word that seems to include its spiritual idolatry, moral depravity and social misery. A few decades later in 722 BC, the next generation of Ninevites would invade the northern tribes of Israel and brutally crush them. The prophet Nahum describes Nineveh as "the city of blood, full of lies, full of plunder ... piles of dead, bodies without number, people stumbling over the corpses" (Nahum 3 v 1, 3). Indeed, there are stone carvings in the British Museum in London today depicting the savage ferocity of the Assyrians (until Nineveh was eventually destroyed by the Babylonians in 612 BC).

It seems that Jonah wasn't disobedient to God's command because he was terrified of their violence, so much as because he was horrified that the Lord would send a prophet to such a sadistic people! We might feel similarly doubtful about a proposal to take the gospel to the Taliban of Afghanistan, or the red light district of Amsterdam, or the filthy rich of Chelsea and New Jersey. *Haven't they brought God's wrath upon themselves?*

Among the significant cities of the Bible, *Jerusalem* was clearly God's city of *righteousness*, illustrating God's promise of heaven; *Babylon* (where the tower of Babel had earlier been built) was the city of *pride*, illustrating God's condemnation of arrogant idolatry; *Sodom and Gomorrah* were the cities of *immorality*, illustrating the severity of God's wrath upon unrepentant unrighteousness; but *Nineveh* was the city of *mercy*, embodying God's passion to save the wicked of all nations—including those we struggle to love! But why did the LORD need to save the people of Nineveh anyway?

Because "its wickedness has come up before me" (Jonah 1 v 2). The wickedness of Nineveh, London and our own village, town or city, offends God because he's sovereign everywhere! Let me explain: I don't really care how messy the bedrooms of teenagers in other people's houses are. But the carnage in the bedrooms of some of my own children has always distressed me because they are *my children living in my home!* And since everyone in the world is created and loved by God, and is living in his world, *everyone's wickedness offends him.* It's as if the wickedness in Nineveh and in all our private lives, however secret and hidden we might have imagined it to be, has been done right in front of his face! Human sin is not only damaging to other people (needing their forgiveness) but deeply offensive to God (needing his forgiveness).

But what is so bad about sin?

Many of us are raised to arrogantly wonder if God should learn to be a bit more tolerant and forgiving? Most think that God should weigh up our good deeds against our bad deeds, and then conclude that most of us have plenty of good to outweigh the bad. Only a few tyrants like Hitler, Stalin and Pol Pot, and a few murderers like Charles Manson, Harold Shipman and the Yorkshire Ripper, should go to hell. But the primary offence for which all humanity in every time and place stands condemned to hell isn't tyranny or murder; it is *neglect* of God.

Many feel that it's unfair for God to punish those born at a time or in a place in which they are unable to hear of Christ in the gospel, such as ancient Aborigines, people born in North Korea or into a strict Hindu community, or the residents of a city like Nineveh. However, Romans 1 makes clear that everyone is aware that God exists from the grandeur of creation. But people of all nations have always suppressed that knowledge of God (Romans 1 v 18-20). We habitually either accept a reinvention of God by the religious ideologies of our culture, or we redesign him ourselves to suit our preferences, declaring boldly, "I like to think of God as...". We call this faith—but God calls it idolatry. Or we even pretend he doesn't exist. People of all nations accept this to avoid submission to the living God and so to be free to indulge in the autonomy and immorality we desire. God hasn't been hiding. But we've slammed the door in his face in various ways. Let me illustrate how serious this is…

Imagine two newly-qualified school teachers, Matt and Tom, starting their first jobs and looking for cheap accommodation. To their delight, a family friend, a wealthy business man with a stunning property near their school, offers them his mansion. "I'll be abroad for a few years on business," he says. "I don't need lots of money—so please enjoy my mansion for £10 a month." The friends are ecstatic. "But do stay in touch," says the owner. "It's a big house and will need careful maintenance, so please respond to my emails, pay the rent on time and have a fantastic time!" The lads move in, each taking one wing of the mansion. Matt is a wild man—a party animal—and soon the east wing is trashed: cigarette burns on the furniture, beer stains on the walls and vomit trodden into the carpets. Everyone knows that when the owner returns, Matt will rightly be kicked out. But Tom is different—quiet and polite. He's so well-behaved that the west wing is spotless. Everyone assumes that the owner will be glad to let Tom stay. But when the owner returns, *he kicks them both out!* Friends of Tom are shocked. But to anyone who asks, the owner explains, "Look, I realise they're different—Matt trashed the place while Tom was tidy. But they *treated me* exactly the same! Both of them utterly ignored me; neither bothered to answer my messages and the house is now seriously damaged. They couldn't even be bothered to pay the small rent I asked for. Since they've so abused my kindness, I'm afraid they can't stay." And no one could quarrel with that.

This story illustrates the different ways we treat God. We live in God's world enjoying his extreme generosity. God expects us to listen to his messages in Scripture, look after his planet and seek his help in prayer. But we ignore and disobey him. Some of us trash our lives—the relational wreckage is everywhere. Others of us are religious and well-behaved. But we have all ignored him, proudly claiming that we have the right to live in heaven. Some of us even ignore God for so long that we declare him dead, and claim the house is now ours! It's no surprise that God will not allow such rebels into his paradise. The tragedy is that we don't realise how *dreadful* life will be without his daily kindness. Jesus consistently taught that life in eternity for unforgiven sinners will be like living for ever in flames, because we've arrived in the presence of the Holy God, who is a consuming fire.

We naturally protest that an eternity in hell seems much too harsh for one short lifetime of sinful neglect of God, because we constantly trivialise our wickedness. But the magnitude of a crime depends in part upon the greatness of the person against whom it is committed. So to kick an opponent in a rugby match is no great crime, but that same kick aimed at Her Majesty, the Queen of the United Kingdom of Great Britain and Northern Ireland, will get you a prison sentence because she is royalty. Since God is of *infinite* majesty, any crime against him is *infinitely serious*. The Lord of heaven and earth does not have to tolerate sinners in his presence any more than we have to tolerate mosquitoes in our tent! Moreover, the time spent in committing a crime does not necessarily indicate its gravity—a murder may be done in a moment of hatred, and every moment of sin is permanent to God. And sadly, there's no indication that unbelievers in hell ever want to stop sinning and turn to God. No one in hell will remain an atheist but all will remain defiant. In truth, my favourite relative, who is popular with everyone for his apparent kindness and infectious sense of humour, is not as lovely in himself as he seems. If he continues to reject God, the Lord will remove from him all the kindness and fun that God has entrusted to him in his character, and his inner soul will be revealed to be bitterly proud and selfishly rebellious against God. Unsaved, we are all *rotten* with sin.

Yet instead of launching an airstrike, God launches an evangelist, for as Peter says, God is "not wanting anyone to perish, but everyone to come to repentance" (2 Peter 3 v 9). The book of Jonah begins with God's words of condemnation but will end with his words of compassion! Indeed in 4 v 2, Jonah explains that this is precisely why he fled:

> *"Isn't this what I said, LORD, when I was still at home? That is what I tried to forestall by fleeing to Tarshish. I knew that you are a gracious and compassionate God, slow to anger and abounding in love, a God who relents from sending calamity."*

In other words, *This mercy is just typical of you, LORD!* Jonah had guessed that Nineveh's wickedness would not only provoke God's frightening wrath but also arouse his compassionate grace.

Since God is sovereign over sinners everywhere, he is offended by sinners everywhere—but he also sends his people from everywhere to evangelise all nations. Perhaps there is a special urgency about reaching the 8000 people groups (nearly half of all people groups in the world) that are reckoned still to be only minimally reached by the gospel of Christ—because they are all sinners he cares about. A young Nigerian Christian pastor recently described to me how somebody in his Yoruba language class in London had criticised him:

> *"How dare you try to spread Christianity among your own people—Christianity has no claim on those of us from West Africa!"*

My friend was able to gently explain that Christ is Lord over all nations—and so he is offended by the sin of all nations, and yet also filled with compassion for all nations. When we evangelise our family and friends, we're not just speaking to them about *our* Lord, but about *their* Lord—introducing them to their Sovereign, who is so offended by their sin that they are left in desperate need of his Saviour; and who still loves them so much that he sends his *reluctant evangelists* to tell them about him.

OUR LORD DIRECTS OUR LIVES FOR HIS MISSION

Read Jonah 1 v 3-10

How can we find opportunities to speak about Christ without being rudely intrusive? Some people seem to be able to strike up conversations and explain the gospel at the drop of a hat. But most of us are more reserved and find evangelistic conversations hard to engineer. Thankfully, God is able to help us…

It seems like centuries ago that I worked as a commercial lawyer in central London, with a Roman Catholic colleague called James. One day, he came to the office with a grubby mark on his forehead because it was Ash Wednesday (signifying the start of the traditional Lent period of self-denial for Roman Catholics). I enquired about the ash and when he explained that he was a Roman Catholic, I cheekily replied with a smile, "So would it be true that you know lots about guilt and not much about forgiveness?" (Perhaps I should explain that in

London my experience has been that Roman Catholics are generally very eager to discuss their faith because they feel uncertain about eternity since their faith is in Mary and the Mass rather than in the finished work of Jesus on the cross.) James was surprised by my cheeky comment, but I'd worked hard at friendships in the office and he agreed to chat more over lunch. After several weeks of discussion, he agreed to come with me to a regular lunch-time church meeting for workers in the city. (I used to hire a taxi to pick up various non-Christian friends from their law firms to come with me.) After a few months of hearing the gospel, he was born again and full of joy in Christ.

When James left the firm, I lost touch with him—until, ten years ago, I discovered that he and his wife, Catherine, had been evangelising and planting churches for many years among the illiterate poor of rural Malawi. When we finally renewed contact in a Skype call, I found that by God's grace they have now planted 35 new churches and just in the last year have baptised 300 new believers! As we talked, we marvelled at the sovereign power of God in using something as tiny and inconsequential as a grubby mark on James's forehead to save so many people in Malawi. We were thanking God for his sovereign control of circumstances and conversations, which now becomes important in the second act of the drama in Jonah 1—in the middle of a storm in the Mediterranean Sea.

Twice, to begin and end this section, we're told that Jonah was fleeing from the LORD (Jonah 1 v 3, 10). Like Adam and Eve in the garden, Jonah tried to hide from God. Amazingly, God didn't strike him down or even replace him with a less troublesome prophet! He let Jonah flee—as did the father of the rebellious son in Jesus' famous parable (Luke 15)—to show Jonah that wherever we run, we'll run into God! When Jonah was told to head east across the desert to Nineveh, he headed west across the sea to Tarshish in Spain. Knowing that the God of heaven made the sea and the dry land (Jonah 1 v 9), Jonah was pretty stupid to do this—but sin always is stupid.

Thankfully for reluctant evangelists like Jonah, God is patient in training us to be fishers of men. Surely Jonah knew Psalm 139, which proclaims God's omnipresence (he is present everywhere): "Where can I go from your Spirit? Where can I flee from your presence?" (v 7)—meaning *You can run, but you can't hide from God*. More of this later.

Jonah had to learn the hard way: in Jonah 1 v 4, the LORD who controls natural forces hurls a violent storm upon the ship, creating a crisis through which he intends to teach Jonah about grace (as he may do in our lives too); in verse 5 the pagan sailors are petrified and, while the prophet of God is sleeping, pray to their powerless gods (just as in London the Muslims pray five times a day while church prayer meetings shrink); so in verse 6, the LORD sovereignly uses the pagan captain to rouse Jonah to prayer, echoing God's earlier command saying, "Arise" (Jonah 1 v 2 and v 6, ESV). So often in public life, unbelievers are waiting for Christians to say something and are shocked to find us sleeping. The captain pointedly comments, "Maybe [God] will take notice of us so that we will not perish" (v 6)—a note of humility that will recur in the unbelievers of Nineveh.

By contrast with this powerless sleeping prophet, the gospels record how Jesus was once sleeping in a boat in a terrible storm. When his disciples called on him for help, Jesus rose up to calm the winds and the waves with a word of divine power (Mark 4 v 39)! This is the divine King to whom we can pray for help in the storms of our lives too.

Circumstances and conversations

In Jonah 1 v 7, when the sailors superstitiously cast lots, the LORD sovereignly directs the outcome to fall on Jonah. Mathematically, lotteries are a waste of money, and spiritually can be dangerous in tempting us into gambling. Even so, Proverbs 16 v 33 says, "The lot is cast into the lap, but its every decision is from the LORD"—for there's nothing random about life under God.

When the desperate sailors interrogate Jonah in verse 8, we finally hear him speak as he confesses, "I worship the LORD, the God of heaven, who made the sea and the dry land" (v 9). Jonah's behaviour horrified these pagan sailors more than it horrified Jonah; they asked, "What have you done?" In other words, *What an idiot you are running away from the LORD, who is the Creator!* Let us pray for God's strength and courage not to behave like Jonah, hiding who we really are from unbelievers, like chameleons—that amazing species of lizard that adapts to its surroundings to stay camouflaged from predators. Many Christians are too much like chameleons at work, indistinguishable from unbelievers—and sadly proud of it.

We do wonder why the LORD still bothers with Jonah; why not let him go, and recruit a better prophet? Indeed, why does God still bother with us when we are so reluctant to talk about Christ to our friends and colleagues? Why not just send angels to evangelise the nations, or drop Bibles and pamphlets from the sky?

Well, first, because God wants us to learn to be evangelistic like Jesus. And since he loves us, he will never give up on us.

And second, because we can translate God's word into the language of our friends better than anyone else. We can be better missionaries to our friends and colleagues than famous evangelists like Tim Keller or Rico Tice, because our friends and colleagues know us and trust us! We can explain gospel truths more clearly for them, answer questions with more understanding of them, and model God's impact in our lives more directly to them, than any celebrity preacher. Indeed, even our ordinary local church ministers can be more persuasive for our guests than great preachers like Kevin DeYoung or Vaughan Roberts on a video, because our pastors know the community our guests live in.

So God persisted with Jonah and he persists with us. But, as with any good parent, his love is now expressed in some painful discipline. Proverbs 3 v 12 explains: "The LORD disciplines those he loves"; and Hebrews 12 v 7 elaborates: "Endure hardship as discipline; God is treating you as his children. For what children are not disciplined by their father?" If we ignore God's great commission to make disciples of all nations, we can expect some loving but painful discipline.

And don't you love how the sovereign Lord uses Jonah's simple testimony to save these sailors—after he's gone, they make sacrifices to God like Jewish believers (Jonah 1 v 16). But Jonah is completely unaware of it because he has been thrown overboard! God had engineered both the circumstances of the storm and the conversation with these pagan sailors to discipline Jonah and save these unbelievers at the same time.

Enjoy the ride!

God's mission to all nations is like a runaway train! Rather than dig our heels in and try to stop it, it would be better to climb aboard and enjoy the ride. Instead of resenting the challenges at our church to invite neighbours to Christmas carol services or friends to mission events, and hiding until the challenge goes away, it would be better to join in and enjoy the ride. And never despair if you don't see much fruit from your conversations about Jesus—God can use the things we say to help save people long after we've forgotten what we talked about. Indeed we may not know until we get to heaven.

To this end, it's worth us preparing and practising our own gospel testimony for any opportunity that God sends. For example, Jonah's testimony in 1 v 9 was "I am a Hebrew and I worship the LORD, the God of heaven, who made the sea and the dry land". If we translate this into the testimony of a Christian today, we might say, "I am a Christian and I follow Jesus (the crucified Galilean), who is Christ (the promised Saviour-King) our Lord (our divine Creator), because he came as our King, died for our sins, rose to rule and will return to judge".

Why not ask your unbelieving friends to allow you to practise with them? I have often used and encouraged groups I train to use the "Two Ways to Live" presentation of the gospel (matthiasmedia.com.au/2wtl/). They have often reported that their friends and colleagues have been glad to allow them to practise their presentation on them, leading to great evangelistic conversations. It is hugely encouraging to know that our Lord the Evangelist still directs the circumstances and conversations of our lives today. I've had many good conversations in taxis when I have prayed for the opportunity—often persuading the drivers to download a free Bible app onto their phones to read a Gospel for themselves.

And we are never too old to have a go! My dear Father is 83 and has been a Christian since his youth. He now has cancer and is rapidly declining in health, so he lives with my beloved mother (who has dementia) in sheltered accommodation. He has felt disappointed that through declining strength he has failed to establish a Bible study among his fellow residents. But an opportunity to confess Christ finally came recently when a local church-plant sent a team to speak at a Christmas lunch event. Throughout the talk my dad was praying for an opportunity to say something. When the service ended, he stood up and addressed his fellow residents, saying:

> *"I'd like you all to know that I agree with everything that preacher just said! I've been following the Lord Jesus since 1947 and there hasn't been a day when I have regretted it. I am pretty sure that I won't be here next Christmas, but I am not afraid of dying because I believe that Jesus will take me to heaven. So if you would like to know how to be saved and come to heaven, please tell me because I would love to explain it to you!"*

He sat down; his fellow residents apparently burst into spontaneous applause, and my dad went back to his room and wept with gratitude for the opportunity. He's an old man who can hardly breathe—but he took the opportunity that the divine Evangelist crafted for him to "do the work of an evangelist" (2 Timothy 4 v 5).

Knowing that God directs the circumstances and conversations of our lives in this way means we can live freely, waiting for evangelistic opportunities without having to be weird or intrusive. For the LORD of Jonah, who directs seemingly random circumstances and chance conversations, can use the testimony of even the most reluctant evangelist, like Jonah, to save people of all nations today.

OUR LORD SAVES THROUGH HIS SACRIFICIAL SUBSTITUTE

Read Jonah 1 v 11-16

How exactly can a holy God save sinners from all nations without compromising his justice? If sin is so serious, then how can God possibly just forgive any of us?

This third act of Jonah chapter 1 recounts the wrath of the LORD, expressed in a violent storm hurled upon the ship, being satisfied by the "death" of his prophet. This points forward to the hill of Calvary outside Jerusalem, where Christ volunteered to die for us to satisfy the wrath of God towards us because of our sin. But in observing these parallels, especially if we are familiar with them, let's beware of diminishing the immense cost of Christ's suffering to his Father in heaven.

A few weeks ago, a Christian friend of ours buried his 16-year-old son, Freddie. Freddie had died unexpectedly and suddenly in the prime of his life. At the funeral service, Freddie's dad, a distinguished surgeon, helped carry his son's coffin into the grand chapel of Wellington School, which was crammed with a thousand mourners. In an extraordinary and emotional tribute, he then explained how being Freddie's father had taught him so much about God's tender love towards us. And he ended by explaining that the anguish of watching his beloved son Freddie die in hospital had taught him a bit more of what it cost God our Father in heaven to watch his Son, Jesus, die in our place on a cross—suffering the horrors of the hell that his people deserve, so that we never have to! Of course, there was not a dry eye in the church as the stunned audience heard this man's courageous faith in the midst of such intense grief. Have you realised something of how much our heavenly Father loves you yet?

In Jonah 1 v 12, Jonah admits his blame for this terrible storm and volunteers to die. The contrast with Jesus, of course, is that Jesus our King accepted responsibility for the behaviour of other people. He died for the sinners from among our rebellious race that the Father had chosen ("elected") to give him from before the foundation of the world ("given" to Christ and "predestined" for heaven; see John 6 v 39 and Ephesians 1 v 4-5, 11).

In Jonah 1 v 13, the sailors, "did their best" to save themselves but couldn't, any more than our best moral efforts can save us from condemnation under God's law on the day of judgment that will take place when Christ returns one day (Romans 2 v 16).

Eventually, in Jonah 1 v 14, they cry out for God's mercy for what they must now do. (They use terms pointedly absent from the lips of the Jewish leaders who later condemned Jesus, our sacrificial substitute, to death.)

"Please, LORD, do not let us die for taking this man's life. Do not hold us accountable for killing an innocent man, for **you, LORD, have done as you pleased.***"*

(Jonah 1 v 14, bold text mine)

These sailors recognised that this sacrifice was a necessary part of the LORD's sovereign will—just as the death of Jesus, killed by unjust and wicked men, was God's plan to save sinners without compromising his justice. Isaiah predicted, "It was *the LORD's will* to crush him and cause him to suffer" (Isaiah 53 v 10), and Peter proclaimed at Pentecost, "This man was handed over to you by *God's deliberate plan* and foreknowledge; and you, with the help of wicked men, put him to death by nailing him to the cross. But God raised him from the dead" (Acts 2 v 23-24). Wicked men put Jesus to death, but God used their wickedness to accomplish his salvation plans.

So in Jonah 1 v 15, "then they took Jonah and threw him overboard, and the raging sea grew calm". With a delicious irony, the sailors didn't know that God would save Jonah; and Jonah didn't know that God would save them.

But, as the wind died down, the sailors could see that Jonah's sacrifice had satisfied the wrath of the LORD.

And God's awesome power in calming the storm brought the ship's crew to simple Old Testament saving faith: "The men greatly feared the LORD, and they offered a sacrifice to the LORD and made vows to him" (Jonah 1 v 16), just as Jonah would later make his vows. He didn't yet know, as he must have later discovered in writing these memoirs, that those pagan sailors had now joined the people of God.

How may we be saved?

We may fret about the shallowness of their understanding, but the behaviour of the sailors is described in the language of Israelite worship. Jesus taught that the simplest faith in Christ, even as fragile as a tiny mustard seed, is sufficient to save—because we're not saved by the power of our faith but by the power of God. The LORD saved those sailors through the satisfaction of the LORD's wrath by the sacrifice of the LORD's prophet—just as he can save us, our families and friends, and anyone through simple faith in Christ's death today. What an encouragement this is: a beloved relative on their deathbed may yet turn to Christ when we hold their hands and pray the Lord's prayer with them, or a friend trapped in the family of another faith can still be saved though a simple faith in Christ. But how can the death of God's Son save us from the punishment we deserve?

Let me illustrate with the extraordinary heroism of Bill Deacon, the winchman of an Air-Sea Rescue helicopter operating in the Shetland Islands, northeast of the Scottish mainland. In November 1997, the Green Lily cargo vessel was grounded on rocks and breaking up in mountainous waves. The lifeboats could no longer get to the stricken vessel to save the crew trapped on board. Bill Deacon realised that the only hope of saving the men was to descend from the helicopter himself onto the ship. Once on the deck, in cyclonic conditions, he attached each of the ten crew to his winch and, in his place, they were raised to safety. But as the last man was rescued, Bill Deacon himself was swept off the ship by a wave, and his body washed up a few days later. He was posthumously awarded the George Medal for his courage.

In the same way, Christ came down from heaven to rescue those in peril. He came to be our King, or captain, so that he could be our representative, taking our place on a cross, accepting the punishment we deserve... all because he loves his Father and loves us so deeply. *Christ became one of us in order to swap places with us*: so he was treated as if he were us on the cross for our sin (and suffered our pain and shame and punishment in hell)—so that we can be treated as if we were him (and accepted into heaven as God's holy children).

Many wonder why Jesus had to die—can't God just forgive and forget? For example, the brilliant but atheistic British scientist Richard Dawkins wrote in his best-selling book *The God Delusion* of the death of Jesus for our sins on the cross in these scornful terms: "I've described atonement, the central doctrine of Christianity, as vicious, sadomasochistic and repellent. We should also dismiss it as barking mad." He just couldn't see that this divine "madness" is what the Bible calls love!

A few weeks ago I had the joy of preaching at my own son's wedding. I recalled that as a teenager he once lost his temper and punched a hole in his bedroom wall. He was mortified by what he'd done and came downstairs in tears to confess with shame the damage he'd caused. Of course, my wife and I forgave him immediately. But... there was still a hole in the wall! Someone had to pay for it. In the same way, when we come to our Lord confessing our sin and pleading for forgiveness, he delights to forgive us our sin. But somebody had to take the consequences of breaking God's law, or God would be the unjust liar who doesn't punish sin after all—a God who allows us to damage other people and rebel against him without consequence. Someone had to pay—but we could never survive paying for ourselves. So God himself volunteered to pay for us on the cross in the bloody humiliation and hell that justice requires—because he loves us so passionately.

In the simplest terms, this was a *swap*—Jesus was treated as if he were us (punished as a rebellious sinner) so that we can be treated as if we were him (qualified for heaven as a righteous son of God).

For more on this, see Appendix: "The gospel" (page 137).

Blinded by your grace

Somebody once observed the following: for God to allow such a sacrifice for us is grace; for God to provide such a sacrifice for us is amazing grace; for God to become that sacrifice for us is grace beyond measure!

Indeed, the south London grime artist, Stormzy, who was declared to be BBC Music's Artist of the Year 2017 for his debut album *Gang Signs & Prayer*, has released an extraordinary track celebrating God's grace (and revealing his Pentecostal church roots), which is called "Blinded by your Grace".

If we are to be effective in evangelism, we have to understand this glorious swap—both to feel the wonder of it in our souls as the driving motivation of our mission and to explain it clearly to unbelieving friends, colleagues and others in language they can understand.

The three acts of the storm drama of Jonah chapter 1 all proclaim that the God of heaven, who made the sea and the land, graciously exercises his sovereignty over all nations in saving sinners, from all nations and cultures, through the evangelistic testimony and self-sacrifice of God's prophet. We can discover how Christ has done both for us in the Gospels. So let us prepare our testimony for when our heavenly Father, who directs all our circumstances and conversations, opens up an opportunity to witness to this living Lord and loving Saviour. And let us join a church-planting team or volunteer to be trained in cross-cultural evangelism—so that we can tell the nations, whether in the city where we live or on the other side of the world, how God has given himself sacrificially in swapping places with us. Because *God is the sovereign evangelist*—and if he could use a reluctant rebel like Jonah to save those pagan sailors in the midst of a raging storm... he can use us too.

OUR LORD IS ALWAYS THERE

Read Jonah 1 v 17 (it won't take long!)

Have you ever been afraid that you've gone so far away from our Lord, rebelled so badly or for so long, that it just isn't possible for God to take you back now? Or has a family member, friend or colleague sunk so deep into a sinful lifestyle, and travelled so far from the word of God and the people of God, that it seems impossible to imagine how the Lord could ever reach them again? Then this little verse will be music to your ears, because it demonstrates that our Lord can rescue his people however far away they've gone, and however low they've sunk, because the God who rescued Jonah is *everywhere*!

To quickly recap: the book of Jonah begins, "The word of the LORD came to Jonah son of Amittai: 'Go to the great city of Nineveh and preach'", much as Christ commanded us, "Go and make disciples of all nations" (Matthew 28 v 19). But instead of obediently heading east across the desert to Nineveh, Jonah disobediently headed west across the sea to Tarshish—much as we flee from myriad opportunities to evangelise our friends, support church plants or engage in cross-cultural mission. The Lord disciplines those he loves, and so he hurled a raging storm at Jonah's ship to reveal his wrath, but ultimately to educate Jonah in the joy of his saving grace. Rather than repent, the stubborn rebel told the sailors to throw him overboard to his death! By avoiding suicide, he forced the sailors to take responsibility for his death. But these sailors cried out for mercy, recognising the Lord's sovereignty over them, and threw Jonah into the sea. God then saved them by the sacrifice of his prophet, which appeased his wrath— just as today he saves us by the sacrifice of Jesus, which has appeased his wrath towards us.

As the storm died away, and the ship sailed on, Jonah, who was presumably not a great swimmer (swimming lessons were not part of the school curriculum in ancient Israel), would have thrashed around for a while until he was utterly exhausted. Then he would have begun to sink down into the Mediterranean Sea to drown. In Jonah 2, we will discover that as he was engulfed by the waters, and brought by distress to the end of his pride, Jonah finally surrendered to God in his heart, yielding up a desperate cry for help. And he was instantly swallowed whole by a huge fish or sea creature (in Jonah 1 v 17 the original language doesn't specify). Plucked from a watery grave in a most extraordinary way by God, who was right there to save this rebel at the last possible moment.

The LORD is always there

In this crisis Jonah experienced one of God's most precious attributes: his *omnipresence*. Psalm 139 v 7-10 proclaims, "Where can I go from your Spirit? Where can I flee from your presence? If I go up to the heavens, you are there; if I make my bed in the depths, you are there. If I rise on the wings of the dawn, if I settle on the far side of the sea, even there your hand will guide me, your right hand will hold me fast." Even in the hidden depths of the Mediterranean, unseen by anyone else in the world, the LORD was right there to save him!

So let me briefly blow your mind: the living God is spirit and so cannot be contained or avoided because all of him is everywhere; he's invisible, immeasurable and uncontainable (unlike pagan conceptions of local deities). He is said to be "immense" in that he doesn't occupy space—so he is never stretched or divided. Indeed, God's centre is everywhere but his circumference is nowhere. So all of his being is personally present in his "simplicity", maximally alive in all his transcendent attributes everywhere simultaneously, not by multiplying himself or dividing himself but by being fully everywhere. Nothing and nowhere in the universe exists except by God's personal presence to sustain and govern it. If you travel to the farthest star of a trillion galaxies to examine the tiniest particle of rock, you would find God fully there sustaining that particle in every nanosecond of history designed for it by him. So God is our constant and personal environment, keeping our heart beating—until he decides it will stop.

God is present to exert his presence variously as he chooses—as a fire may give warmth or light or cause destruction without ever ceasing to be fire, so God is present to provide our daily needs, enlighten us by his word or punish his enemies in his hell. God can intensify his presence to delight his people, for example in the Garden of Eden, in the tabernacle and temple, in a local church, and by filling us with his Spirit as his word dwells richly in us (Colossians 3 v 16; Ephesians 5 v 18). He is more intensely present yet in heaven, and fully in Jesus.

Astonishing as it is, this omnipresent Lord shrank and condensed himself down to a few tiny cells in Mary's womb, in order to reveal himself to us in the skin-and-bone category of a human life, a life that can be described in Scripture, comprehended by us all—and was given for his people on a Roman cross!

God can intensify his presence to punish—for hell is not the devil's torture chamber; it is where sinners who have suppressed their knowledge of God and the gospel must experience the justice of God's fiery holiness. Without being clothed in the righteous holiness of Christ, unbelievers will arrive in the presence of God as if they were landing on the surface of the sun naked. It seems that God will not light the fires of hell—for he is the fire in hell, present to judge and not to bless.

And since God is everywhere, he is inescapable. There's no privacy or secrecy from him, even in the depths of our own hearts. Our most private gossip, hidden jealousy, secret lusts and forgotten cruelty—all of these are said, thought and done permanently in his presence. The fourth-century theologian, Augustine wrote:

> *"Since there is one even more deeply inward than yourself,*
> *there is no place where you may flee from an angered God*

> *except to a God who is pacified. There is absolutely no place*
> *for you to flee to. Do you want to flee **from** him? Rather flee*
> ***to** him."*   *(Augustine, Expositions on the Psalms,*
> *on Psalm 74, bold text mine)*

If anyone reading these words is currently running, or tempted to run, from God, please learn from Jonah—you can run but you can't hide! Instead of fleeing from him in rebellion, flee to him for mercy.

Could you ever love maggots?

When I empty our rubbish bins in summer, I sometimes find a horde of filthy wriggling maggots at the bottom. I cannot imagine ever loving them enough to become one of them to die for them. Although we are certainly more precious than maggots, the distance between us and maggots is smaller than the difference between God and us. Christ is infinitely greater than us—and yet he died for us. It's almost obscene. He loves us so much that he became one of us so that he could suffer what we deserve, so that we can be in heaven as he deserves—to be united together for ever with him as his beloved and beautiful bride.

A man recently converted at our church was once a soldier in a Scottish regiment, then a prison officer, and now is a security guard. When interviewed, he admitted:

> *"I've done terrible things in my life—but when I think that*
> *God sent Jesus to die for me on that cross, and then came to*
> *find me and save me, I find it overwhelming—and I still cry*
> *every day!"*

When Jonah finally cried out for mercy the LORD was right there to rescue him:

> *"Now the LORD provided a huge fish to swallow Jonah,*
> *and Jonah was in the belly of the fish three days and*
> *three nights."*   *(Jonah 1 v 17)*

And in the cramped, slimy darkness of the fish's stomach, presumably gulping in fetid air stinking of rotting fish, Jonah realised that against all odds he was safe! It's obvious that such a bizarre salvation can only be due to God's amazing grace. There are dubious Victorian reports of a young whaler called James Bartley, who in 1891 fell into the mouth of a sperm whale. Eighteen hours later, with permanently mottled skin, he was apparently cut out of its belly on the deck of a ship called *Star of the East*.

Thankfully, we don't need such tales to trust the Jonah account. We know it is history, and not myth or allegory, because:

1. Matthew and Luke both record Jesus treating it as factual, and we trust him.
2. The account reads as historical narrative and nothing like a myth or parable.
3. God can do what he wants: if he resurrected Jesus from his tomb, he can certainly keep a man alive for a few days in a fish!

Consider three wonderful things about this astonishing rescue:

a. **Consider how utterly lost Jonah was.** As the storm died away and the ship sailed on, Jonah was alone somewhere in the Mediterranean Sea, utterly beyond the help of anybody... except the God who made the sea and the land. His precarious situation illustrates how lost each of us were when God found us: we were drowning in sin—just one car crash or skin cancer or heart attack away from death, beyond the help of anyone... except this Lord. So however wicked an unbeliever has been, or however far a believer has strayed, we can never be too lost for God to find us.

b. **Consider how perfect this saviour was.** The phrase "and the LORD appointed" (ESV)—this is literally "had appointed"—emphasises that God had previously arranged for this particular giant fish to take this particular gulp of water in this particular spot in the sea at this particular moment in history—to ensure that Jonah was swallowed alive by a living submarine! This was an absurd but perfect saviour, demonstrating to Jonah, to the Ninevites when they heard of it, and to us who now read about it, that this was God's miraculous grace. A rescue by a passing ship would have left him indebted elsewhere; but a ridiculously big fish can only be due to the ridiculously big grace of the LORD. In the same way, even before creation, God had appointed for us an absurdly weak but spiritually ideal Saviour—smashed up on a cross for our sins to complete the perfectly obedient Christian life we all need to qualify us for heaven. All because he loves us! However lost we have been, Jesus is the ideal Saviour for us.

c. **Consider how inactive Jonah was.** God didn't empower Jonah to swim for shore like an Olympic athlete, or provide some passing driftwood for him to paddle home, giving Jonah cause to boast. No, Jonah is carried to safety, like a patient in an ambulance, saved entirely by God's merciful kindness and nothing of his own effort. As Paul later writes, "It is by grace you have been saved, through faith—and this is not from yourselves, it is the gift of God—not by works, so that no one can boast" (Ephesians 2 v 8-9). Indeed, while Jesus explicitly draws an analogy only between Jonah's survival in the fish and his own survival in the tomb, I think we can also enjoy the simple parallel with our being saved "in Christ". For when God calls us through his gospel to faith in Christ, we're spiritually united with him. So we share in his experience of resurrection from the dead, spiritually now and physically one day, in Christ, just as Jonah was brought from death to life in the fish.

In Christ alone

Allow me to illustrate: when Harry Kane (an England soccer player) scores a goal, England supporters yell, "We've scored!" Only one man kicked the football, but we all benefit, because he represents us. So the Bible says we've died, we've been raised, and we've been seated in heaven "in Christ" (Romans 6; Ephesians 2); we live "in him". We are incorporated into his privileges as Son of God: so as the LORD preserved Jonah in the fish through the perils of the deep until he was spewed safely onto the beach, so God now preserves us through the perils of life and death and judgment "in Christ", until we are delivered safely onto the shores of the new creation. Never forget that, like Jonah being carried in a fish, or lambs being carried by a shepherd, or exiles being carried on eagles' wings, we are being carried home to God. Or, as the teaching of the European Reformers on our salvation has famously been summarised, we have been saved through *faith alone*, by *grace alone*, in *Christ alone*, according to *Scripture alone* to the glory of *God alone*.

If the Lord who can save like this is everywhere, then no one is beyond his grace. Indeed, every local church is a trophy cabinet of God's far-reaching grace. Even in my own church family there are those whom God has saved who you might have assumed were far beyond salvation: a young mum who grew up in North Korea in the family of a senior army general; a retired SAS colonel; a successful young same-sex-attracted businessman; a young mum who grew up in an Indian Muslim family; and even some working-class Brits raised in hardbitten secular cynicism! So don't give up praying for sinners and speaking to them about Christ when you can—because the omnipresent God, who saved Jonah, can reach anyone drowning in sin. For no one is beyond the love of the God who is everywhere. And however badly believers rebel—whether like King David, who committed adultery and murder, or like the prophet Jonah, who fled from the Lord—the divine Evangelist is always there, willing to rescue them.

Jonah tried to run away from the LORD, but "the LORD provided a huge fish to swallow Jonah". So never give up on the lost, however far they've run and however low they've sunk. Because God knows exactly where they are and is right there to rescue them, from the moment they repent and cry out to him.

OUR LORD'S GRACE IS TRANSFORMING

Read Jonah 2 v 1-7

What effect does God intend his salvation to have upon us? What impact will God's grace have upon our hearts? Well the transforming power of God's saving grace could not be more clearly demonstrated than in the prayer of Jonah from the belly of the great fish when he realised that he had been saved. Let's notice the order here: it is not that Jonah changed his attitude and so earned God's salvation; rather, God's saving grace is what transformed Jonah's attitude.

To put this more carefully, there is a biblical order to our salvation (sometimes referred to as the *ordo salutis*). This includes:

- First, God predestined and elected many sinners for salvation; then…
- He sent Jesus to die for us on the cross; next…

- He sent someone to explain to us what he has done in his gospel; through which...
- His Spirit called and regenerated us to respond with repentant faith; and then...
- God justified and adopted us as his children; so that...
- We start praying with joyful gratitude.

The reason God wants us to understand this is so that we don't start telling people that praying like Jonah is how we save ourselves. Rather, we start praying like Jonah when God has saved us—for this is how his grace begins to transform our hearts.

Transforming the heart of a reluctant evangelist

Let's consider how the heart of this reluctant evangelist was transformed into the heart of a willing evangelist. As the great fish swam around in the Mediterranean Sea, Jonah was bizarrely trapped in its belly. Any passing boats would have had no idea of the drama unfolding beneath the waves. Though presumably struggling for oxygen, bewildered in the darkness and desperately uncomfortable, Jonah, the rebellious prophet, realised that he had been rescued and was now being miraculously preserved by his Creator, "the God of heaven, who made the sea and the dry land" (Jonah 1 v 9).

In Jonah 2 v 1-9 of these memoirs, Jonah vividly recalls his prayer of thanksgiving from within the fish, which is similar to Moses' song after Israel was delivered safely across the Red Sea (Exodus 15), and is full of quotations from psalms that Jonah must have learned as a boy and studied as a prophet. But there is more here than gratitude. There is a repentant humility and a sacrificial willingness to serve God (Jonah 2 v 9). Presumably, one reason that God made Jonah wait for those terrifying three days and three nights inside that fish (1 v 17), in addition to creating a parallel with Jesus' burial in his tomb, was to give this period of incapacity for prayerful reflection (as he may give us an opportunity for prayerful reflection during a period of sickness or unemployment). The text is clear that Jonah was only "released" from the fish when he finally recognised that "salvation comes from the LORD". His heart had been transformed by God's grace (though not completely, as we shall see).

Jonah's prayer reveals how deeply he was changed by his dramatic experience of God's grace, as the slave-trader John Newton was changed when saved through a terrible storm, and wrote those beautiful words:

> *"Amazing grace, how sweet the sound*
> *That saved a wretch like me!*
> *I once was lost but now am found;*
> *Was blind, but now I see."*

In the accounts of both Jonah and John Newton, we see the truth of Paul's teaching that the grace of God "teaches us to say 'No' to ungodliness and worldly passions, and to live self-controlled, upright and godly lives in this present age" (Titus 2 v 12). If we want obedient children, respectful teenagers, sexually disciplined students, faithful spouses, generous workers, prayerful retirees, and above all evangelistic Christians, we must keep proclaiming the saving grace of God towards us in Christ! For it is God's salvation that transforms hearts—spiritually in generating life, motivationally in fuelling our gratitude, behaviourally in learning that holiness is not just an absence of evil but the presence of evangelistic love, and above all theologically in realising that we have been saved for a purpose. Paul explained that Christ "gave himself for us to redeem us from all wickedness and to purify for himself a people that are his very own, eager to do what is good" (Titus 2 v 14), especially in evangelism.

Jonah's prayer

Let's see how God's saving grace changed Jonah:

> *"From inside the fish Jonah prayed to **the LORD his God.**"*
> *(Jonah 2 v 1, bold text mine)*

Jonah knew that, having fled from the LORD, it was the LORD who had sent the storm and now rescued him from the sea—and so he acknowledges that this LORD must still be "his God". In verses 2-7 he recalls his prayer of thanksgiving. There are three recurrent themes before he arrives at some big conclusions in verses 8-10:

a. **He realised his need.** The trauma of the storm and being cast overboard had finally convinced Jonah of his weakness and the madness of running from the living God. He had finally cried for help, "from deep in the realm of the dead" (v 2)—for the ocean was almost his tomb—and from "the depths" (v 3)—for he'd sunk beyond all hope of human rescue. He remembers that he was completely overwhelmed: "engulfing waters threatened me, the deep surrounded me; seaweed was wrapped around my head" (v 5)—he was trapped and drowning. Indeed, "the earth beneath barred me in for ever … [in] the pit" (v 6)— he had been imprisoned by death and condemned to hell; he realised "my life was ebbing away" (v 7)—for in losing his battle for air he was losing his grip on life itself. Jonah was faced with the grim reality of his impending death and condemnation by God.

Facing imminent death, whether in a car accident or a cancer ward, can often spur an unbeliever to consider their eternity. I recall a most wonderful series of conversations with a woman who discovered that she had just three weeks to live. When I visited her in hospital, she agreed to skip the small talk and get straight to understanding the gospel of Christ, crucified and risen for our salvation. When we said goodbye, she promised to pray to Christ for forgiveness, and I promised to tell her family and everyone at her funeral of the Saviour she came to embrace in her last days on earth. I am really looking forward to seeing her again in heaven. Indeed, you might say that in reality we're all like Jonah frantically treading water, until one day we will sink into death, perhaps in a hospice bed with our family gathered around, as we gasp for breath; and then the monitor will flat-line and we'll be dead. *Are you forgiven and ready to meet your Maker?*

Jonah knew he was in *serious trouble with God*. "*You* hurled me into the depths" (v 3)—the sailors were only doing God's will. "*Your* waves and breakers swept over me"—God had determined his fate. "I have been banished from *your* sight" (v 4)—God had excluded him from heaven. Such language is familiar from many psalms, such as Psalm 130 v 1: "Out of the depths I cry to you, LORD". The first aim in evangelism, and the work of God's Spirit through God's law, is to convince people of their sin and their need of God's mercy—that's why we must ask them to respond to the gospel by *saying "sorry"* to God. So, first, Jonah had realised his need; next...

b. **He cried out for help.** Many people think that to be saved from hell we must just paddle faster than other people—try harder to be better than others and have enough good deeds and religious performance to outweigh our failures and filth. But even if some people are better swimmers than others, everyone drowns in death eventually. As with the penitent thief crucified with Jesus, it was obvious to Jonah as he sank in the sea that his time was up. Trying to improve our performance sufficiently to qualify ourselves for heaven is always a doomed exercise—and now it was too late for Jonah go to synagogue, too late to give more money, too late to learn more Bible. All he could do was humble himself before the LORD and cry out for help—"I *called* to the LORD ... I *called* for help" (v 2); "I *remembered* you, LORD, and *my prayer rose* to you" (v 7). These words urge us all to issue our own SOS distress signal to God in prayer: to urge others to respond to the gospel by *saying "please help"* to God. Have you ever actually responded to what Christ has done from the depths of your inner soul, crying out,

"Help—please save me"? Look what happens when you finally do…

c. **He received mercy.** In verse 2, Jonah says, "He answered me … you listened to my cry"—even in the depths of the sea the LORD heard the jumbled thoughts of his desperate soul. And in verse 6 he says, "You … brought my life up from the pit"; that is, *You've saved me from death and hell.* Notice that God heard Jonah from the midst of his discipline. If any of us has been living in rebellion—perhaps tangled up in the seaweed of greed or immorality— it is never too late to call upon our heavenly Father for mercy. I think of two men saved recently: one was discovered by his young wife to have been visiting prostitutes for years; another, tangled up in gambling, stole £40,000 from work, and his wife knew nothing until the police turned up to arrest him. Both men, drowning in shame, cried out to the God who loves us so much that he sent his Son to die for our sins—and wonderfully experienced his forgiveness and power to change them. And when Christ has saved us from our captivity to sin, opening the prison cell to lead us out from our various addictions, even though we are sometimes tempted back into the filth of our old lives and return to the squalor of our old lifestyle, Jesus keeps coming back to lead us out of the filth in repentance. Until one day, he will finally lead us out for good and take us to heaven, closing the door of sin behind us for ever. As Jonah prayed, we need to pray and to encourage others to pray, *saying "thank you"* to

God for his saving grace in Christ, who came to swap places with us on the cross.

Sorry, please, thank you

In our evangelism we must urge people to respond to the gospel as Jonah did, when he confessed his need, cried out for help and was thankful for mercy. Or, to put it simply, we need to respond to God's grace by praying, "*Sorry* for my sin. *Please* forgive me. *Thank you* for your saving grace in Jesus."

But how is such saving grace possible? In Psalm 69 we read the description of the death of God's coming Saviour-King in these terms:

> "*Save me, O God, for the waters have come up to my neck.*
> *I sink in the miry depths, where there is no foothold. I have*
> *come into the deep waters; the floods engulf me. I am worn*
> *out calling for help.*"   (Psalm 69 v 1-3)

This psalm looked forward to our Saviour, Jesus, experiencing the death that sinners deserve under God's wrath in our place, described in terms of a death by drowning, such as nearly engulfed Jonah. Jonah was delivered from drowning in his sins, because Christ was drowned for our sins on the cross of Calvary. This is why people saved by grace, like Jonah and us, respond to the gospel in prayers that say, "*Sorry… please… thank you*".

This experience of God's grace had transformed Jonah, from heartless rebel into willing evangelist. And if we lack his new willingness to evangelise, we need to revisit Christ's death for us described in the Gospels, to reconsider the transforming grace of Christ—for as Paul writes later, "Christ's love compels us" (2 Corinthians 5 v 14).

OUR LORD IS KINDER THAN IDOLS

Read Jonah 2 v 8-9

Do you ever feel arrogant asking someone to leave their religion and follow Jesus? Especially if they are likely to face hostility and even violence from their families for abandoning the faith of their family?

A Palestinian friend of mine living in Jerusalem, once a Muslim and member of the PLO (Palestinian Liberation Organisation) but now a Christian, explained to me that he regularly gets death threats from Hamas (an Islamic political and military organisation).

When he first became a Christian, he took bread to his village and tried to tell his people the gospel of Christ; but his former friends machine-gunned his car and warned him that they would behead him if he ever returned. But, he once boldly told us:

*"I have no regrets in turning to Jesus; when I was a Muslim,
I had no peace with God. Now I am a Christian, I can go to
sleep at night knowing I am at peace with God through Jesus
for ever, even if they kill me tomorrow!"*

Like my friend, we need to learn what Jonah realised: that
clinging to false gods is worthless. Until we get that clear, we
will never persist in persuading others to turn to Christ. In
Jonah chapter 2, Jonah is recalling his prayer from inside the
belly of the great fish, as he realised that he had been saved in a
bizarre but effective living submarine! He now arrives at some
vital conclusions—after which he will be ready for his mission
and will be spewed out onto the beach.

*"Those who cling to worthless idols turn away from
God's love."*   *(Jonah 2 v 8)*

For unlike living for our Lord, *there's no kindness to be found in
serving idols.* But we may think that idols are not a problem for
us in the 21st century. So what exactly is idolatry?

The nature of our human condition is normally described
in the Bible in one of two main ways:

a. As our ***failure*** *in righteousness before God*—for which
   we need to be "*justified*" (or declared righteous by God
   in the *righteousness of Christ* completed at the cross),
   to be qualified by him for heaven (as explained, for
   example, in Romans).

b. As *our **departure** in worship to idols*—for which we
   need to be "*reconciled*" (or at peace with God through
   the *blood of Christ* shed at the cross), to be friends with
   God (as explained, for example, in Ephesians).

These two aspects of God's salvation correspond with the two dominant worldviews among sinners today:

a. What we might call the "*performance*" worldview of older generations and many non-Western cultures, concerned with social hierarchy, family responsibility, duty, good works and honesty. The gospel challenges this religious view today, as it did the Jewish outlook of the first century. The condemnation of God's law exposes our humbling need for our Messiah to die in our place to suffer for our failures and to complete a perfect life of righteousness for us, so that we can be justified in his righteousness. (We see an example of this in Paul's evangelism of Jews in Acts 13).

b. What we might call the "*rights*" worldview of Western cultures flooding younger generations in our cities via the internet. This is the confident assertion of personal autonomy—our right to choose our own objects of worship. This worldview is narcissistic and pluralistic, and resurrects the ancient worship of created things called *idolatry*. The gospel challenges this rebellious worldview with the resurrection of Jesus from the dead to judge our ignorant neglect of our Creator in worshipping idols. (See Paul's horrified response to the idolatry of Athens in Acts 17 for an example of this.)

Such idolatry is where we give our devotion to something other than the living God in three ways:

a. By making visible images of God, such as Aaron's golden calf (Exodus 32) or Greek Orthodox icons.

b. By worshipping alternative deities such as Baal, Vishnu or Allah.

c. Where we misdirect our worship towards good things given by God instead of God himself. For example, we may be devoted to our career and status, or our wealth and leisure, or our pleasure and sexual ecstasy, or our children's education and achievement, or our reputation and popularity, or our own image of health and beauty—all of which are making good things into our god things.

How to tell which god we worship

Whatever we sing on Sundays, we can tell which god we really worship by how we spend our spare time, what we're devastated by losing, and where we turn in trouble. So if I drool over television shows about luxury homes and holidays but rarely read my Bible, insure everything I own but rarely give much to gospel work, and throw cash rather than prayer at every problem, then, whatever my friends assume, my god is money.

Tim Keller has written extensively and brilliantly on this subject. He points out that whether we cling to the culturally inherited gods of ancient religions or the chosen objects of modern worship, our idols will be enormously costly, requiring huge sacrifice from us, whether of animals on an altar or of hours in the office. But idol worship is offensive to God because we have foolishly "exchanged the glory of the immortal God for images made to look like a mortal human being" and "exchanged the truth about God for a lie, and worshipped and served created things rather than the Creator" (Romans 1 v 23, 25). And such idols cannot satisfy or save our souls because they're not the living God. Jonah recognised that those who cling to serving idols miss out on the eternal joys of being saved and sustained by the grace of our living and loving Lord.

A resolution to live with sacrificial thankfulness

> *"But I, with shouts of grateful praise, will sacrifice to you.*
> *What I have vowed I will make good."* (Jonah 2 v 9)

Jonah will now sing God's praises and gladly accept the cost of serving him. For Hebrews 13 v 15 says, "Let us continually offer to God a sacrifice of praise—the fruit of lips that openly profess his name"—that is, praising God, to his face in prayer, to believers with encouragement, and to unbelievers in evangelism, whatever the social or physical cost. For us, this may mean some embarrassment and the mockery of friends and family. Let's remember that for our Eritrean brothers and sisters in Christ, it may well mean being locked in a metal shipping container in the desert for weeks until we perish; or in North Korea, it may mean being laid down to have our heads crushed by a steamroller. So let's not be quick to complain.

Jonah has clearly come a long way. He now realises that the Ninevites need saving from idolatry, and he is now willing to serve the LORD sacrificially. Indeed, his prayer ends with the central celebration of the book: "Salvation comes from the LORD" (Jonah 2 v 9). Jonah's experience of saving grace has transformed his heart, and the LORD has prepared Jonah for his evangelistic mission by exposing how much kinder than idols he is. Jonah now realises that God is all about salvation.

Indeed, Jonah is about to discover that God can reach people in the most impossible places and cultures. I have a dear friend called Sergei, who lives in Belarus. He's a church leader and church-planter. As a young man, he fought in Afghanistan with the legendary elite Russian special forces, the Spetsnaz. Once, when visiting his home in Minsk, I was thumbing through his photo album and came across a picture of him and his comrades leaning against a tank in the Afghan mountains. Sergei looked so violent, with ammunition belts criss-crossing his bare chest and holding a machine gun on each hip. He looked like Rambo! But the next photo in the album caught the moment he was baptised in a silly white nightie in a river in Minsk.

I asked Sergei:

> *"How on earth did God save a hardened atheist and communist special forces soldier like you—surely no one could be further from Christ than you?"*

He explained that many men came home in body bags from that campaign, and the mother of one of his comrades had told him to go to church when he got back from the war, and invited Sergei to come with her son. On the agreed Sunday, Sergei turned up at the tiny Baptist church but his friend didn't. So Sergei went in and listened to a little old preacher explain the gospel—and was convinced it was true. He returned next week to hear the message of grace again, and surrendered himself to Christ. What an encouragement that is for all of us, and especially for nagging mums and little old preachers!

But can you hear an ugly note of self-righteousness that still remains in Jonah here? He contrasts "*those* who cling to worthless idols" with himself: "but *I*, with shouts of grateful praise, will sacrifice to you. What *I* have vowed *I* will make good." He still despises Gentiles. Those of us brought up in church culture can easily despise Hindus, scorn Buddhists and even hate Muslims, which, as we shall see, is *not* how God sees people. Jonah still needs to learn the biggest lesson of all that we need to learn in evangelism: *to love the lost.*

He will learn this lesson painfully; for he will shortly witness a whole pagan city turn to the LORD and experience the same saving grace that he has enjoyed in the great fish (and will later hear that the pagan sailors on his ship had already experienced). Perhaps, like some of us, Jonah's experience of grace has made him *willing* to obey the LORD, but not yet to *care* about unbelievers. But at least he has realised the emptiness of serving created things in place of our gracious Creator. We need to believe this for ourselves, or we will never try to persuade unbelievers that they have forfeited the amazing grace that could be theirs in Christ.

OUR LORD'S GOSPEL ANNOUNCES HIS JUDGMENT

Read Jonah 3 v 1-4

What is God's "gospel" (the good news that saves people)?

Some while ago, I studied at a great Bible college in Sydney, Australia. One of the more memorable training experiences was when the renowned evangelist, John Chapman, invited some people who regularly brought unbelieving friends to church, to tell us what kind of evangelistic preaching they wanted to hear. Since John was famous for his hilariously self-deprecating anecdotes as well as his faithfulness to Scripture, we might have expected something about the magnetic power of humour. But the message from each of the "bringers" was the same, and delivered in the bluntest terms—"If I finally manage to get one of my friends to come to church, *you better tell them the gospel!*"

The same thing happened recently in my preaching class for our young Gospel Ministry Trainees. We were discussing some illustrations I was thinking of using in a sermon for a Christmas Carols by Candlelight service, when we're usually rammed with guests. One of our trainees, Pete, piped up nervously, "You are going to explain the gospel, aren't you? I've got some friends coming and I desperately want them to hear it!" He was absolutely right to say something, because too many preachers think that if they're nice and friendly and funny, and avoid saying anything controversial, people will surely want to come back to church and become Christians. Instead, generally speaking in London, we find that if guests have an enjoyable time they might be willing to come back in a year's time, having been not the slightest bit disturbed from their secular beliefs. By contrast, Paul writes, "I am not ashamed of the gospel, because it is the power of God that brings salvation to everyone who believes" (Romans 1 v 16). But many Bible-loving Christians are not very clear about what the Bible itself says the gospel is.

For a more detailed look at God's gospel, please read the Appendix on page 137.

Good news about God's Son

The word "gospel" means a momentous announcement—not good advice or good ideas but good news.

God's gospel is his good news *regarding his Son* (Romans 1 v 3). So if we're not talking about Jesus, even if we are explaining marvellous things about God the Father or God the Holy Spirit or our church, no one can be saved. We see this in the famous verse, John 3 v 16:

- "For God so loved the world" is the *reason* for the gospel;

- "that he gave his one and only Son" is a *summary* of the gospel; and…

- "that whoever believes in him shall not perish but have eternal life" is the *result* of the gospel.

So if we talk about God's love or about eternal life, we are talking of wonderful things but not of the gospel that saves. If we want people to be saved, we must explain what happened when God sent his Son.

To summarise briefly, God's gospel proclaims God's good news that *Jesus is our Lord and Saviour*: that is, who Jesus is (our *Lord*) and what Jesus has done (our *Saviour*).

To expand a little:

Jesus is our Lord: This is to say that *Jesus* (the crucified Galilean) *is Christ* (the long-promised Saviour-King) *our Lord* (the divine Ruler of all) (Romans 1 v 1-4).

Jesus is our Saviour: This is to say that Christ *came as our King* (Mark 1 v 15), *died for our sins* (1 Corinthians 15 v 3), *rose to rule over us* (1 Corinthians 15 v 20-25) and *will return to judge* (Romans 2 v 16).

The simplest way to summarise this saving gospel is one four letter word: "*swap*". God loves us so passionately that he became one of us in Jesus in order to swap places with us on the cross—where he was treated as we should be treated and judged for our sin, so that we can be treated as he should be treated and accepted into heaven as perfect children of God.

We need to get ready for judgment

But some popular gospel presentations and courses don't even mention Christ's return to judge, despite the Bible explicitly saying that judgment is part of God's gospel that saves—for example, "the day when *God judges people's secrets through Jesus Christ, as my gospel declares*" (Romans 2 v 16; see also Revelation 14 v 6-7). Jesus consistently taught that people need salvation from God's judgment, which will launch an eternity of extravagant blessing in his renewed creation for his repentant followers but an eternity of torment in hell for his unrepentant enemies (Matthew 25 v 41). If we only talk of the benefits of being Christians in this life, it may not be so obvious to unbelievers why it is worth becoming a Christian, and we will be tempted to exaggerate the blessings and lie about the costs of following Jesus. Indeed the Bible says, "If only for this life we have hope in Christ, we are of all people most to be pitied" (1 Corinthians 15 v 19). But when we speak of judgment and eternity, it could not be more obvious why it is worth being a Christian. So if we want people to be saved, we will have to find a way to talk about Christ's return to judge.

Now I'm not suggesting that we turn into annoying "hell-fire and damnation" preachers, like one brave but misguided evangelist who for many years, whenever I went to preach at one of our midweek ministries in central London, was standing at the crossroads of Oxford Circus. He would bellow repeatedly through his loudhailer, "Turn or burn!" But everyone avoided him like the plague and no one stopped to speak to him because he seemed so crazy and threatening. Yet it is very striking that the conversion of Nineveh, perhaps the greatest revival in Bible history, began when Jonah faithfully proclaimed God's message of judgment. Let's see what happened...

> *"Then the word of the LORD came to Jonah a second time."*
>
> *(Jonah 3 v 1)*

How *totally wonderful* to discover that our Lord is the God of second chances. Having disciplined and rescued Jonah, God saw no need to issue a nagging torrent of new instructions and warnings. Nor did God give up on Jonah and get someone else more reliable. He simply issued exactly the same command as before. How fantastic that where we've previously failed to love others enough to speak to them about Jesus, when we repent, he'll give us another go—he's the God of second chances. Mind you, the LORD didn't negotiate with Jonah...

> *"Go to the great city of Nineveh and proclaim to it the message I give you."*
>
> *(Jonah 3 v 2)*

Jonah is told to proclaim the message he is given—forestalling every temptation to modify God's word to make it more popular. Nor are we at liberty to remove the pages or twist the parts of the Bible that are politically incorrect in our culture. This would not only be disobedient but ineffective—because if it's not God's word, it won't have God's power to save. Indeed, if people come to church and just hear the world's ideology, they may as well stay in bed and read the secular papers—which is what many Londoners are doing. I'm not for one minute suggesting that we must announce all the most difficult and countercultural Bible doctrines to our guests the moment they arrive in church. It is often wise to reserve more controversial doctrines for careful and extended teaching and discussion in a mid-week context (in London at the moment the most inflammable issues are homosexuality and gender). But I am saying that "we have renounced secret and shameful ways; we do not use deception, nor do we distort the word of God. On the contrary, by setting forth the truth plainly we commend ourselves to everyone's conscience in the sight of God" (2 Corinthians 4 v 2). We must not deny, misrepresent or twist what the Bible says, but, in the right context, teach the truth honestly, clearly and carefully, with as much kindness and understanding as possible. Jonah had tried rebellion before—and it brought some firm discipline in which he nearly drowned! So this time…

> *"Jonah obeyed the word of the LORD and went to Nineveh.*
> *Now Nineveh was a very large city; it took three days to go*
> *through it."*   *(Jonah 3 v 3)*

Jonah obeyed and made the long journey to the famously violent and idolatrous city of Nineveh in the emerging powerhouse of Assyria. This city mattered, not just because of its political and commercial status, but (see Jonah 4 v 11) because there were so many unsaved people there. So what did this visiting speaker proclaim?

> *"Jonah began by going a day's journey into the city,*
> *proclaiming, 'Forty more days and Nineveh will be*
> *overthrown.'"*   *(Jonah 3 v 4)*

It is very unlikely that this is all he said. After all, Jesus later says that Jonah's survival in a fish was a sign to Nineveh in the same way that Jesus' resurrection is a sign for us today. So presumably Jonah had to explain his experience of the LORD's deliverance (perhaps illustrated by some very strange burns on his skin from the stomach acid of the fish) just as we must explain the evidence for the resurrection of Christ provided for us in the Bible.

But the only thing God wants us to know about the message through which he brought this great revival, is this blunt warning about God's judgment: "Forty more days and Nineveh will be overturned". Can you picture that? Imagine arriving in Islamabad today, walking into the central square in front of the mosque and announcing, "The Lord God of Israel has told me to warn you that in a month you'll be destroyed"! Jonah's obedience was certainly brave! In most Western cities today, announcing the wrath of God to unbelievers who know little of Jesus sounds mad—more likely to deter people than draw them. But if we don't explain the danger we are all in, how will anyone be persuaded of their need of a Saviour?

The great preacher Martyn Lloyd-Jones, used mightily by God in times of revival in Wales, once declared:

> "I'm not afraid of being charged, as I frequently am, with trying to frighten you, for I am definitely trying to do so. If the wondrous love of God in Christ Jesus and the hope of glory is not sufficient to attract you, then, such is the value I attach to the worth of your soul, I will do my utmost to alarm you with a sight of the terrors of hell."
>
> (Iain H. Murray, D. Martyn Lloyd-Jones, Vol. 1 (Edinburgh: Banner of Truth, 2008), p 216)

Without using medieval language or being unwisely hasty or self-righteous, we need to find appropriate ways to warn people of the wrath to come. In practice, I find in London that if I accuse other people of their sins, they are deeply offended; but if I simply describe my own sinfulness, and confess that I've realised that I would be in serious trouble with God without a Saviour, others are more than ready to agree. Jonah announced God's judgment and... something amazing happened:

> "The Ninevites believed God." (Jonah 3 v 5)

They recognised in the warnings of Jonah the word of the LORD and the whole city turned to the LORD in repentance. This wasn't just because of a shock-and-awe preaching tactic— for when Stephen proclaimed judgment in Acts 7, he was stoned to death. Nor was this just a uniquely miraculous day when one sentence about judgment converted a city—but will never do so again. I assume Jonah took his time to tell his story and win his audience, to recount something of the history of the LORD's dealings with Israel, including previous times when the LORD had carried out his warnings and inflicted severe judgment, such as on Sodom and Gomorrah. Our text is clearly just an executive summary of Jonah's teaching. But God only tells us that Jonah proclaimed judgment because, unlike Jonah (who, we suspect, was very glad to announce judgment), most of us find this so difficult to do.

The kindness of warnings

From the beginning, the devil has been spinning the lie he told Eve in the Garden of Eden: *You will not die*"(Genesis 3 v 4). But she did die. Most people in London find it shocking to think that anyone still believes in the reality and eternity of hell, let alone that without Christ they are going there. Yet Jesus, the man who is God and alone knows the plans of the Almighty, and who suffered on a cross to save us from hell for heaven, repeatedly insisted that hell is a shocking reality. In the parable of the net, Jesus told his disciples, "This is how it will be at the end of the age. The angels will come and separate the wicked from the righteous and throw them into the blazing furnace, where there will be weeping and gnashing of teeth" (Matthew 13 v 49-50).

Jesus talked like this because he doesn't want any of us to go there. It's an expression of his love. It's like a roadside warning that reads, "Tiredness can kill—take a break" or a mother yelling at her active toddler, "Don't go near the road or a car will kill you!" Such warnings are expressions of kindness and not hatred. We ourselves need to understand, and persuade others to understand, that the truth is helpful, even when it is uncomfortable to hear. For example, imagine three patients with heart disease being asked into the doctor's surgery after their scans and x-rays. "Well," said the doctor, "I do have some good news for you, but you won't realise it's good news until I first tell you some bad news, okay?" The patients were full of trepidation and remained silent. So the doctor continued: "All of you have heart disease because you've been chain-smoking for more than thirty years and now, unless each of you has major surgery, you will soon suffer coronary failure and be dead within a year". "Outrageous!" shrieked the first patient. "How could you be so nasty? I came in here expecting some reassuring encouragement, and you've just accused me of failing to stop smoking, and made me feel terrible. You're the cruellest doctor I've ever met." And she stormed out.

The second patient responded quietly but with menacing fury: "How dare you! Who do you think you are, accusing me of failing to stop smoking and criticising my heart? You don't even know me! I'm sure I'll find other doctors to tell me I'm fine—after all, I'm not as bad as some smokers I know. And I feel fine. You're the most arrogant doctor I've ever met." And he too left the room.

The third patient sat quietly for a moment. "Doctor, I know I've failed to stop smoking and it's quite a shock to hear I need surgery. But thanks for telling me the truth. I'm so relieved to hear the good news about an operation that can save my life—please tell me about it." Don't we want to be like the third patient—willing to hear the uncomfortable truth and be saved?

It's no accident that preachers like Jonathan Edwards were greatly used by God in the 1730s Evangelical Revival in New England. For Edwards not only proclaimed the attractive beauty of Christ but also the dreadful torments of his judgment. Here are a few words from his sermon, "The Eternity of Hell Torments":

> *"Consider what it is to suffer extreme torment for ever*
> *and ever; and to suffer it day and night, from one year to*
> *another, from one age to another, from one thousand ages*
> *to another, and so adding age to age, and thousand to*
> *thousands, in pain, in wailing and lamenting, groaning*
> *and shrieking, and gnashing your teeth; with your soul*
> *full of dreadful grief and amazement, with your bodies …*
> *full of racking torture, without any possibility of getting*
> *ease; without any possibility of moving God to pity by your*
> *cries; without any possibility of hiding yourselves from him;*
> *without any possibility of diverting your thoughts from your*
> *pain … Consider how dreadful despair will be [in such*

*torments] to know assuredly that you never, never shall be
delivered from them. To have no hope."*

It's too harrowing to go on. Of course, it's usually wise to delay
telling unbelieving friends about the wrath to come until they
trust us enough to hear it from us, and we must think carefully
about the language we use. So, rather than self-righteously
accusing others, we may find it helpful to say something like,
"I don't know about you, but I've realised that I'm in serious
trouble with God because of my pride and my selfishness and
lust—and because of all the opportunities I waste to be kind
to other people and to honour God". When we explain how
we've realised that we need a Saviour, it is amazing how much
more willing people are to accept that *they* need him too. But
if we don't explain the wrath to come, Jesus will never seem as
marvellous as he is.

Indeed, when unbelievers discover that we believe in
judgment, they are bound to ask why we haven't bothered to
mention it if we claim to care about them. Penn Jillette (of
Penn & Teller magic fame) is an atheist, but said this about
evangelism:

*"I've always said that I don't respect people who don't
evangelise. I don't respect that at all. If you believe there is a
heaven and hell, and people could be going to hell, and you
think it's not really worth telling them this because it would
make it socially awkward ... How much do you have to hate
somebody to not evangelise?! How much do you have to hate
someone to believe everlasting life is possible and not tell them
that? ... If I believed, beyond a shadow of a doubt, that a
truck was coming at you, and you didn't believe it, that that*

truck was bearing down on you, there's a certain point that I
tackle you."

(Jillette, Penn, "Not proselytize",
youtube, Rich Maurer, 13 November 2009)

And if we don't explain God's judgment, then the death of Christ doesn't seem at all wonderful. Imagine walking out of your house and seeing Jesus standing on the other side of the road. Then he yells, "I love you", and throws himself under a truck, so that there's blood all over the road! Well, it's certainly dramatic—but you never asked him to do that. And likewise, telling an unbeliever that Jesus died to show us how much he loves us sounds emotional but completely unnecessary. But if Jesus runs towards you yelling, "I love you" to knock you out of the way of the truck that was going to flatten you, but is killed by the truck in saving you, then you would know that he died in your place because he loves you. God's wrath is that truck—and the torments of our hell are what he suffered on the cross. Now you know how much he loves you.

Tim Keller has helpfully observed that God generally saves secular Westerners when they…

a. hear *sensible truth*;

b. encounter *credible people*; and

c. experience a *deep sense of need*.

This recognises that people are rational, social and distracted beings, and so respond to influences that are truthful, liveable and necessary. It strikes me that the gospel provides all three: the gospel is *sensible truth about historic events* which we must explain clearly in language that people can understand; and churches where this gospel is believed will be *credible people full of kindness and love*; and the gospel also reveals the relevance and necessity of Christ in that it warns us of God's judgment to come. The gospel of the Bible, including judgment, is what unbelievers will need in every age and culture.

On fire!

Of course, the reality of judgment should be a powerful motivation for believers. While Jonah seems to have been driven by a self-righteous vindictiveness, the apostle Paul was driven by compassion:

> *"We must all appear before the judgment seat of Christ, so that each of us may receive what is due to us for the things done while in the body ... Since, then, we know what it is to fear the Lord, we try to persuade others."*
>
> *(2 Corinthians 5 v 10-11)*

Could any of us imagine walking home one night and, looking into the front room of a house in our street, we see that a cigarette stub or burning log has fallen onto some furniture, so that now the curtains are ablaze with flames up to the ceiling, with the family asleep upstairs... and we do nothing? Could we possibly leave the family to burn because we were late for tea or wanted to watch the football on TV? Surely we would hammer on the door, pleading with the family to escape, even if they shout at us to stop bothering them.

So let me tell you an uncomfortable truth: your whole street is on fire! Because your street is filled with people who don't know of the judgment to come or of the loving Saviour who can rescue them. But that's why God has arranged for you to live where you live. I don't know what that means for you—perhaps it means organising a Christmas drinks evening where you invite your church pastor to explain the true meaning of Christmas, or knocking on every door with an invitation to an Easter outreach event, or a summer barbecue where you give your testimony? The one thing I know you can't do is… nothing. The first step to saving grace for Nineveh was that Jonah preached the judgment of God. God's gospel requires us to find a way to do the same. Anything less is just not loving.

OUR LORD CALLS EVERYONE TO TURN IN REPENTANT FAITH

Read Jonah 3 v 5-10

When we engage in evangelism, what exactly are we urging people to do? Or to put it another way, how does someone become a Christian?

For many years, I've been trying to help my friend Jimmy become a Christian. He's a talented professional musician, and tours the world playing with famous rock bands to packed stadiums. To be honest, I'm slightly in awe of him. He's a wonderful husband and dad, but he knows he needs forgiveness for his rebellion against God. He was raised as a Roman Catholic—but this has only made him more aware of his guilt. When he's here in London, I've been chatting and reading the Bible with him, trying to show him that Jesus Christ, crucified for our sins and raised to qualify us for heaven, is the loving Saviour and living Lord he needs. But what am I praying Jimmy will do?

Or imagine this exciting moment. You've been praying for months it would happen. Two non-Christian friends have finally come with you to church. Wonderfully, the minister is finishing an excellent talk and your friends are plainly gripped. He's clearly proclaimed the gospel, with compelling illustrations—that Jesus is Christ our Lord: who came as our King, died for our sins, rose to rule and will return to judge. He now needs to explain simply how to become a Christian. What are you praying he will say? Or if he mucks it up, what are you asking God for an opportunity to say as you head off with your friends to a coffee shop? Especially if one of them claims, "I've always been a Christian" and the other says, "I tried Christianity at school but it doesn't work for me," and you're pretty sure that neither of them was ever truly saved?

So many people think they've tried Christianity (sometimes because somebody told them too early that they were saved) and are now cynical, but in truth they have never been born again. We need to know the answer to the famous question that a prison officer once asked the apostle Paul: "What must I do to be saved?" (Acts 16 v 30). People often use romantic phrases such as "I found Jesus" or "God saved me" or "I came to faith"—but what do these actually mean? How does somebody become a real Christian in practice?

How to be saved

The simple answer is that God calls us through his gospel to *turn in repentant faith*.

Paul told the church leaders in Ephesus, "I have declared to both Jews and Greeks that they must *turn* to God in *repentance* and have *faith* in our Lord Jesus" (Acts 20 v 21).

"Turning" is the language of Old Testament preachers such as Elijah. On Mount Carmel, in his great public battle with the prophets of Baal, Elijah called down fire from heaven, praying, "Answer me, so these people will know that you, Lord, are God, and that you are turning their hearts back again" (1 Kings 18 v 37). And it is the language of New Testament apostles such as Paul, who wrote, "You *turned* to God from idols to serve the living and true God, and to wait for his Son from heaven" (1 Thessalonians 1 v 9-10).

Throughout the Bible, "turning" is a simple way of explaining repentant faith, because repentance and faith are twin aspects of turning around. God wants us to turn *from* sinful idolatry (repentance) *to* worshipping Christ (faith). So repentance and faith are two sides of the same coin—turning.

So sometimes we read of Jesus and Paul requiring *repentance*. For example, to a crowd in Galilee, Jesus insisted, "Unless you *repent*, you too will all perish"; and to the intellectuals of Athens, Paul proclaimed, "He commands all people everywhere to *repent*" (Luke 13 v 5; Acts 17 v 30).

But on other occasions Jesus and Paul required *faith* (often translated "belief"). Jesus said, "For God so loved the world that he gave his one and only Son, that whoever *believes* in him shall not perish but have eternal life"; and Paul told the Philippian jailor, "*Believe* in the Lord Jesus, and you will be saved" (John 3 v 16; Acts 16 v 31).

Notice that we're saved not so much by our repentant faith as by Christ through our repentant faith (which the Spirit of God creates through his gospel)—just as an exhausted swimmer at Bondi Beach in Sydney, being carried to safety on a lifeguard's surfboard, is being saved by the lifeguard through lying down on his board, because the lifeguard told him to.

Repentance means changing your mind

The word translated as "repentance" means to "change your mind", but this is deeper than just an intellectual agreement. It isn't saving repentance just to *understand* the gospel, or *feel* the power of the gospel, or even to *agree* with the truth of the gospel. It means changing our minds to the depth of our will (the intentions of our minds) and the core of our desires (the affections of our hearts), which will always be *expressed in costly behavioural change*. That's why John the Baptist insists on repentance being expressed not just in words but in actions: "Produce fruit in keeping with repentance" (Matthew 3 v 8).

Repentance is not promising to be perfect—because our sinful nature remains in us and we will keep failing. But repentance is promising to try—a genuine commitment to change. This is why Paul tells King Herod Agrippa, "I preached that they should repent and turn to God and *demonstrate their repentance* by their deeds" (Acts 26 v 20). We are not saved by our changed behaviour—we are saved by Jesus. But we are saved *for* changed behaviour; and if we don't intend or desire to change, we're not really repenting—and are not yet saved.

This is so important because it explains why so many people who assumed they were Christians later seem to "fall away" when, in truth, they were never saved. In his parable of the soils (Matthew 13), Jesus explains that only time will tell if someone is truly saved; for although in some people the gospel is quickly snatched away by Satan before it penetrates at all, in others the gospel seems to grow briefly, but is then scorched by the cost of opposition. Then in some the gospel seems to grow for a while, but is eventually choked by the competing desires and concerns of this world before it ever really takes root (perhaps because these people were raised in a family or culture where everyone uses Christian language, or because they were told too quickly that they were saved). Only in some does the gospel sink deep down in genuinely repentant faith, but these people will be hugely fruitful in evangelistic multiplication. This is exciting because we can reassure the person who thought they'd tried Christianity and given up that they haven't yet experienced the excitement of rebirth, which God gives to those who genuinely turn to him in repentant faith. And we can challenge the person who claims always to have been a Christian—that no one is a Christian until they've consciously turned to God (whether or not they were ever baptised).

Faith means turning to trust in God

The word for "faith" (often translated "belief") means to *trust* or *depend* upon something or someone. When unbelievers say, "I wish I had your faith", they haven't realised that they already exercise faith when they get on a train trusting it to take them somewhere, or take medicine prescribed by the doctor they trust. They have our faith, but don't yet place their faith in Christ for salvation. Such faith is created in spiritually dead unbelievers by the Holy Spirit through the gospel, for "faith comes from hearing … the word" (Romans 10 v 17). Christian faith is not an irrational confidence in fantasy, as Western culture often claims. The gospel we believe is true and real—evidenced with more than enough proof in the Bible (John 20 v 31) including verifiable eyewitness accounts, logical arguments, detailed predictions and convincing signs. That's why the method by which people come to saving faith throughout Acts is not emotional *manipulation* that bypasses the mind but *persuasion* that addresses the mind; for example, Paul "reasoned with them from the Scriptures, explaining and proving ... arguing persuasively about the kingdom of God" (Acts 17 v 2-3, 19 v 8).

This word "faith" is massive! When I first arrived at Bible college in Sydney, the principal kindly picked me up from the airport and gave me supper. As we washed up afterwards, he asked me a brilliant question: "What word do you think best summarises the Christian life?" Well, I floundered around, coming up with all sorts of embarrassing suggestions until he finally put me out of my misery. "How about *faith*?" he gently suggested. Of course! "Faith" summarises our way of *knowing* God (believing what he reveals about himself), our way of *salvation* by God (believing his gospel promise), our way of *pleasing* God (trusting his word enough to obey it), our way of *experiencing* God (feeling the spiritual impact of his words) and our *confidence* in God's word even when we don't feel it or see it ourselves:

> *"Faith is confidence in what we hope for and assurance about*
> *what we do not see."* (Hebrews 11 v 1)

The word that best summarises the whole Christian life is certainly faith.

What does repentant faith look like in practice?

This all sounds fine in theory. But *what does turning to God in repentant faith look like in practice?* That is where Jonah 3 is so helpful. For when the godless people of Nineveh heard Jonah proclaiming the judgment of the LORD, they responded to his message with repentant faith! And we know this is what God wants from us because we read, "When God saw what they did and how they turned from their evil ways, he relented and did not bring upon them the destruction he had threatened" (Jonah 3 v 10). If we want God to show us this same mercy, these four stages are how we turn to him in genuine repentant faith:

a. **They believed God's word** (Jonah 3 v 4-5)—"Jonah began by going a day's journey into the city, proclaiming, 'Forty more days and Nineveh will be overthrown.' The Ninevites believed God." In believing Jonah's message as words from God, the residents of Nineveh were just like the Thessalonian Christians to whom the apostle Paul later wrote, "When you received the word of God, which you heard from us, you accepted it not as the word of men, but *as it actually is, the word of God*, which is indeed at work in you who believe" (1 Thessalonians 2 v 13). *This is the cognitive aspect of repentance.*

The same thing happens in cities all over the world today. When we read God's word with a colleague during a lunch-break, or explain it to friends in a coffee shop, or proclaim it to a congregation in church, God can open the spiritually blind eyes of sceptical pagans to recognise God's truth, not in our words but wherever we explain the words of the Bible. This has two implications:

First, it's sobering that God doesn't always do this. I find it heartbreaking that some of my wider family and friends have heard many clear evangelistic talks, but they say, "Sorry, I can't see it!" Paul explains that there is nothing wrong with God's word (so don't change it), but there is something wrong with unbelievers (so ask God to help them), for "the god of this age [Satan] has blinded the minds of unbelievers, so that they *cannot see* the light of the gospel that displays the glory of Christ". They are like blind people staring straight into a brilliant searchlight and declaring that everything is dark. When we were unbelievers, we too were blinded in our minds by Satan and we were guilty of welcoming his lies. Paul then explains how people can be enlightened by God: "What we preach is not ourselves but Jesus Christ as Lord [the gospel] ... for God, who said, 'Let light shine out of darkness,' made his light shine in our hearts to give us the light of the knowledge of God's glory displayed in the face of Christ" (2 Corinthians 4 v 4-6). When our Creator so chooses, his Spirit shines the spiritual light of his word into our hearts so that we see God... in Christ... in the words of the gospel. So we must not change the gospel but pray for unbelievers: that, in his mercy, God will enlighten guilty sinners like us through his gospel—knowing that he is not obliged to do so and often doesn't. And...

Second, the encouragement here is that God used a reluctant evangelist like Jonah with an unpromising message of judgment to save a whole pagan city. So don't be frightened if you don't feel remotely impressive or clever enough when you are trying to explain the gospel. Out of love for unbelievers (but not to impress them with how worldly we are) we will work hard to do this to the best of our ability in the most supportive environment we can provide. So preachers will work hard to prepare faithful, well-applied expositions, support teams will work hard at logistics and media, caterers will labour over refreshments for guests, and everyone will plead with God in prayer to open blind eyes. For unbelievers will surely conclude that our message is trivial if we don't try to do things as excellently as we can. But we'll probably be very conscious of our failings and clumsiness—many of us struggle to explain the gospel clearly and we may not have a very exciting life or home to share; at church our musicians may not be very talented and our Bible-teachers may be very ordinary—but God's gospel can save a whole city in one go.

In fact, God likes to use our weakness. Paul writes, "We have this treasure [the gospel] in jars of clay" (we are as ordinary as cheap clay pots or common plastic bags) "to show that this all-surpassing power is from God and not from us (2 Corinthians 4 v 7). God likes unbelievers to realise that he is the Saviour and not us, and that we evangelise because the gospel is true and not for any personal benefit. Unbelievers are often repelled by exaggerated spin and loveless bling; the treasure we have to offer them, the precious gift we have, is not our brilliance but the life-saving gospel of

Christ and him crucified. If the Lord could open the eyes of these pagan Assyrians through Jonah, he can save our friends through us explaining his gospel.

b. **They humbled themselves** (Jonah 3 v 5)—"A fast was proclaimed, and all of them, from the greatest to the least, put on sackcloth". If you'd wandered into downtown Nineveh in those days, the normally bustling markets and crowded food stalls would have been deserted because everyone was fasting—it was like a city under siege. Everybody, even the wealthy, had discarded their fashionable wardrobes and looked like beggars, shuffling around anxiously in the sackcloth of mourning and penitence. Their dress code indicated their genuine regret for their idolatry and immorality, and a deep humbling of their pride.

This is the *attitudinal* aspect of genuine, repentant faith. It wasn't the superficial religious version of humility: turning over a new leaf and trying to be less arrogant in order to earn God's grace. They genuinely regretted their sins, admitted their guilt, and accepted that they deserved punishment. When the psalmist says, "You save the humble" (Psalm 18 v 27) and we repeatedly read, "He/God … shows favour to the humble" (Proverbs 3 v 34; James 4 v 6; 1 Peter 5 v 5), we're not being told that self-humbling is the way to impress God. Real humility is recognising some horrifying truths: we have failed, we are filthy, we are guilty and we deserve punishment—in fact, we should be in hell right now.

c. **They turned from their sin** (Jonah 3 v 8)—The Assyrian king had commanded, "Let them give up their evil ways and their violence"—so as you wandered around, the usually busy temples and backstreet brothels were all boarded up; and there was no sign of the violence described by historians—no prisoners of war with their ears and noses cut off being skinned alive. This was the *behavioural* aspect of their repentant faith: a genuine commitment of minds and hearts to behave differently—they were turning from their sin.

d. **They pleaded for mercy** (Jonah 3 v 8-9)—the king also commanded his people, "Let everyone call urgently on God … Who knows? God may yet relent and with compassion turn from his fierce anger so that we will not perish." They genuinely begged for mercy—this is the *reliant* aspect of repentant faith. They recognised that their prayers guaranteed nothing. There was none of our common presumption that treats God like a slot machine, as if he is obliged to forgive, like the genie in the lamp who must grant us our wishes. As Christians, we can trust God to forgive all who repent because he has wonderfully promised to do so: "If we confess our sins, he is faithful and just and will forgive us our sins and purify us from all unrighteousness" (1 John 1 v 9). But such confidence in God's grace is different from presumption, which forgets that we deserve to go to hell.

We're in a different place now

Some who grew up in Christian families may not be able to remember when they turned to God. Or we may have come to repentant faith over a period of time rather than on a particular date. It's been helpfully said that we can cross a national border either consciously on the ground at a checkpoint or unconsciously in the sky in an aeroplane, but either way we are now in a different country than before. Some of us know a specific time and others don't; but even if we don't know exactly when it happened, we do need to be consciously living by repentant faith now, which is to be in a very different place to where we once were.

If there's no great change in us, it's probably because we're not yet Christians. Jesus said, "No one can see the kingdom of God unless they are born again" of the Spirit (John 3 v 3); and James explains, "He chose to give us birth through the word of truth", his gospel (James 1 v 18). Being born again is an essential change, evidenced in turning to God in repentant faith such as we witness in Nineveh, expressed in prayer.

To summarise with an easily remembered answer to the question, "What must I do to be saved?" I find it useful to urge people to pray, *"Sorry... thank you... please"* as follows:

> *"Dear God,*
> *Sorry for my sin (repentance).*
> *Thank you for sending Jesus to die*
> *and rise again for me (the gospel).*
> *Please forgive me and help me to*
> *follow Jesus from now on (faith).*
> *Amen."*

Have you ever prayed this kind of prayer yourself? Why not pray it now to be certain?

Indeed, you may recall that this is the same kind of prayer that Jonah himself was praying from inside the fish—for this is the kind of prayer we will pray throughout our Christian lives. For though we don't need to repeatedly become a Christian, our direction of travel will for ever be the same as when we began.

So this is what we must urge unbelievers to do. Those who are born again through the gospel must *turn to God in repentance and faith.*

OUR LORD HAS PROMISED TO RELENT

Read Jonah 3 v 10

This little verse raises a lot of questions: If God relented and did not bring the destruction upon Nineveh that he had threatened, does that mean that he might change his mind about other things too? Could he decide not to save us—or not to judge the world after all? Indeed, if we pray a lot, can we get God to do what we want—or is prayer a waste of time? How is the sovereignty of God related to our prayers?

We've seen that Jonah isn't about Jonah and a whale but about the LORD and a reluctant evangelist. We've seen that God is the global Evangelist who is *sovereign* (Jonah 1), *gracious* (Jonah 2), *merciful* (Jonah 3) and *compassionate* (Jonah 4), saving a city of 120,000 spiritually clueless pagans through his gospel message, despite their wickedness and despite the reluctance of his prophet, because "Salvation comes from the LORD" (Jonah 2 v 9).

The immense encouragement of Jonah is that no one, whether as rebellious as Jonah or as pagan as Nineveh, is beyond the mercy and grace of God. What an encouragement for reluctant evangelists this is.

Jesus later described himself as "the sign of Jonah" (Matthew 12 v 39), for as Jonah was raised by God from a fish to preach the gospel to *his* wicked generation, so Jesus was raised from his tomb to proclaim the gospel to *our* wicked generation. Jesus refused to do miracles on demand for the cynical Pharisees, but he did recognise the need of the lost for a sign—for evidence that his message was from the living God. Jesus said the sign that unbelievers in every generation and culture will need is the "sign of Jonah". Notice that it's not Jesus' resurrection itself that is the sign of Jonah—but the teaching of the resurrected Jesus that is the sign. For just as the Ninevites heard Jonah's teaching but didn't watch Jonah being spewed out of the great fish, we hear Jesus' teaching but can't watch Jesus emerging from his tomb. But as Jonah's extraordinary experience authenticated his message to the Ninevites as coming from God to them, so Jesus' resurrection authenticates his teaching, proclaimed by the apostles and now preserved in the Bible, as coming from God to us. We need to take the teaching of Jesus, God's resurrected preacher, to the nations. His teaching is the sign that they need.

Moreover, Jesus wants us to repent like the Ninevites, for Jesus declared, "The men of Nineveh will stand up at the judgment with this generation and condemn it; for they repented at the preaching of Jonah, and now something greater than Jonah is here" (Matthew 12 v 41). Jesus is warning us all that if the Ninevites were willing to turn to God when they heard an unimpressive prophet like Jonah, we should be aware that God will judge more severely those who refuse to turn to him when they hear the teaching of Jesus.

Now, wonderfully, we can rejoice in God's response to the repentant faith of Nineveh:

> *"When God saw what they did and how they turned from*
> *their evil ways, he relented and did not bring on them the*
> *destruction he had threatened."*   *(Jonah 3 v 10)*

It was when God *"saw what they did"*—not just heard what they said or sang or prayed, but saw how they *turned* from their evil ways with repentant faith—that he had compassion and "did not bring on them the destruction he had threatened". God was wonderfully merciful and did not inflict upon them the destruction he had threatened.

But this now raises a problem for the thoughtful Bible student: because it sounds as if God changed his mind when the Ninevites prayed. Although that initially sounds like an exciting encouragement to pray, that starts to sound worrying because God could change his mind about great promises he's made. The Bible reassures us, "God is not human, that he should lie, not a human being that he should change his mind. Does he speak and then not act? Does he promise and not fulfil?" (Numbers 23 v 19) God never needs to change his mind because his knowledge and wisdom are always perfect. God is said to be *"immutable"*, meaning that he's unchanging and utterly reliable in his character, will and promises. Indeed, God cannot change, because if he did, he was either imperfect before that change or imperfect after that change—and in either case he wouldn't be God!

But God's immutability also causes a problem for the faithful evangelist, because it sounds as if there's no point in praying for unbelievers to be saved or even for unbelievers to pray for mercy—because God will never change his mind. What is the point of any prayer if God never changes his mind? There are two wonderful truths here about the marvellous Lord of heaven and earth, who is evangelising his world:

a. *God's "immutability" (unchanging character) is of great comfort to us in trusting his promises, especially the gospel.* People change constantly because our human nature is inherently unstable. We have fickle emotions and weak characters, so we are all unreliable to some degree. Most of us will have been hurt in the past by the infidelity of people we've trusted. But God never changes—and so he's never unreliable in his words and promises. He's never unstable or inconsistent— leaving us uncertain about what he wants or how he'll react. He is repeatedly compared to a *solid rock* on which we can build our lives with secure confidence. For example, Jesus said, "Everyone who hears these words of mine and puts them into practice is like a wise man who built his house on the rock" (Matthew 7 v 24). Indeed, Jesus practised what he preached when he later explained that he is building his own church on the rock of the gospel (Matthew 16 v 16-18). God is therefore the *impregnable fortress* in whom we can take refuge for safety, help and comfort: "The LORD is my rock, my fortress and my deliverer; *my God is my rock, in whom I take refuge*" (Psalm 18 v 2).

b. *When God is described as answering prayers in terms such as relenting from bringing destruction, he's not changing his mind but is faithfully keeping his promises to relent exactly when he has planned to do so.* So God had already promised *explicitly* in Jeremiah 18 v 7-8, "If at any time I announce that a nation or kingdom is to be uprooted, torn down and destroyed, and *if that nation I warned repents of its evil, then I will relent* and not inflict on it the disaster I had planned". This is exactly what God did when the Ninevites called out to him in prayer. Being utterly consistent with that promise, the LORD didn't change his mind, but he did relent and withhold his judgment as he always planned to do. And in 1 John 1, we are promised that "If we confess our sins, he is faithful and just to forgive us our sins and purify us from all unrighteousness" (1 John 1 v 9). So when anyone turns to God in repentant faith, he will keep his stable promise to relent and show mercy.

The point of prayer

But if God "knows what you need before you ask him" (Matthew 6 v 8) and "does not lie or change his mind" (1 Samuel 15 v 29), then… what is the point of prayer? In his masterly chapter on prayer in his famous *Institutes*, the great 16th-century Reformer John Calvin clarified six wonderful reasons for prayer, which we can apply to our evangelistic enterprise:

Dependence—so that our hearts become inflamed with *"burning desire to seek, love and serve him … and become accustomed in every need to flee to him as to a sacred anchor"*.

That is, by praying we learn to depend upon God for the success of our evangelistic efforts and therefore to pray to him before we speak to people; and we will consequently want to give good time for congregational prayer before we launch our church outreach initiatives.

Purity—so that our hearts don't nurture desires and longings of which *"we should be ashamed to make him a witness"*. So by praying we learn to purify our desires so that we don't do our evangelism to look impressive, expand our tribe or exploit unbelievers but for the benefit of others and to the glory of God.

Gratitude—so that we learn to *"receive his benefits with true gratitude"*. By praying we learn to be content with what our Father provides, not boasting when things go well but giving him the glory when people are saved, not exaggerating or despairing when the fruit of our evangelism is modest but being content with whatever evangelistic fruit God chooses to give us.

Appreciation—so that we *"meditate upon his kindness more ardently"*. In prayer we learn to appreciate God's faithful generosity and so to recognise his blessing when we have great conversations about the gospel and when people are saved at church.

Enjoyment—so that we may *"embrace with greater delight"* the things we receive from praying. In prayer we learn to enjoy without inhibition the good gifts our Father provides and so to celebrate without embarrassment when people turn to Christ.

Trust—so that we learn to *"confirm his providence"*. In prayer we learn to trust God for our daily needs and so not to worry too much about what does and doesn't work when we are trying our best.

Calvin summarised prayer as *"digging up the treasures"* that are promised to us in Scripture; and so while there are no specific promises that particular people will become Christians, we can ask Christ to keep his promise to be with us to the end of the age when we're trying to make disciples (Matthew 28 v 19-20).

As Christians we find that it is our regular experience that God delays giving us the things he plans to grant to us until we ask for them in prayer. God had always planned to give them to us when we pray—in order to strengthen our confidence in him. So from our perspective, *things happen when we pray.* Indeed, he teaches us to pray by withholding his gifts until we pray—*so pray lots!* As a loving parent will teach a toddler grateful dependence by withholding gifts until they ask properly, so God teaches us to pray in dependence, purity, gratitude, appreciation, enjoyment and trust by withholding blessings until we ask him. A godly archbishop was once asked by a sceptical journalist if answers to prayer were simply coincidences. He wisely replied, "I don't know— it's just that when I stop praying, the coincidences seem to stop happening".

If you are an unbeliever, pray now for mercy, for God has promised to forgive you if you do. And *if you are a believer*, pray for unbelievers you know by name, for God has promised to save them if they turn to him in repentant faith—and *he may well be waiting until you pray for them before he saves them* because he wants to show you that he loves you. My father has a wise but simple message stuck to the top of his computer screen. It reads, "PRAY YOU FOOL!"

So Nineveh was not destroyed as Jonah had threatened. The reason God could do this justly would not become clear until Christ died on the cross for the sins of Nineveh as well as ours: the lightning rod attracting to himself all the bolts of God's wrath, draining to the last drop the acid cup of God's judgment! The wonderful news of Jonah 3 v 10 is that the Lord is willing to relent and show mercy towards all who, like the people of Nineveh, turn to him and pray for mercy.

OUR LORD CHALLENGES OUR CULTURAL PREJUDICE

Read Jonah 4 v 1-4

How committed do we feel to cross-cultural mission, whether in our community or around the world? Could we rejoice if our church grew to become predominantly West African or South Korean or South African? Why are we so opinionated about the style of music, the length of the sermon or the clothes that people wear in church? These are just cultural issues.

Racial and cultural prejudice are delicate issues. But I recall a highly amusing conversation with some Dutch and Palestinian Christians in Jerusalem recounting how some American and Spanish visitors had admitted their serious cultural suspicions of each other. The Americans had agreed, "We were shocked at how much alcohol you Spanish Christians drink!" To which the Spanish replied with some amusement, "Well, we were shocked at how much make-up you Americans wear!" I was still quietly struggling with being hugged and kissed by the Palestinian men.

Christians rejoice that in Christ, we are "all one in Christ Jesus" (Galatians 3 v 28). One of the chief privileges of being a Christian pastor has been to travel, and so to discover that Christians in the completely different cultures of Chile, Belarus, Kenya and South Korea love the same Lord and believe the same Bible as I do. But in the nitty-gritty of congregational life, and a church-planting network committed to social and ethnic diversity in a multicultural city like London, where less than half the population are now white British, bruising cultural assumptions and painful blindspots are harder to address. We recently hosted some young Koreans in our home who'd lived in London for a decade but explained that ours was the first English home they had ever been in. Ouch! One of our young black pastors recently pointed out to me, "The effect of racial prejudice significantly impacts black people's lives here in London: education, employment, housing, health care, criminal justice, and so on. Christians need their pastors to help them deal with these traumas and challenges so they can respond in godly ways, but very few know how." He is right and we have so much to learn. But Christians are brothers and sisters in Christ, who have the Spirit of God, who applies to all our hearts the spiritual unity that already exists in Christ.

Cross-cultural evangelism is hard because it requires a love for unbelievers that will challenge our cultural prejudices—especially those we're not aware of. But we have to learn how to do this because Christ has commanded us all, "Go and make disciples of *all nations*" (Matthew 28 v 19), and as global migration grows, most of us can access many nations without leaving our own neighbourhoods. In Britain, it is often harder to cross socio-economic "class" boundaries than ethnic boundaries. Students and young professionals from many nations may look different but share the same globalised cultural assumptions and aspirations; whereas the urban poor and privileged elite will find it extremely difficult to build meaningful relationships with each other in which evangelistic conversations can take place. But Paul wrote, "Though I am free and belong to no one, I have made myself a slave to everyone, to win as many as possible ... I have become all things to all people so that by all possible means I might save some" (1 Corinthians 9 v 19, 22). Jonah 4 brutally exposes the prejudice of our hearts in the self-righteous vindictiveness of Jonah.

God's concern and Jonah's displeasure

We've seen that the heart of the book of Jonah is the prophet's celebratory realisation from within the belly of the great fish in Jonah 2 v 9, that "salvation comes from the LORD"—for God's holiness is evangelistic. Now chapter 4 begins with a glorious proclamation of the LORD's character as the central confession of the second half of the book, concerning God's grace towards pagan Nineveh: "You are a gracious and compassionate God, slow to anger and abounding in love" (Jonah 4 v 2). This matches the central statement of the first half concerned with God's grace to Jonah: "I worship the LORD, the God of heaven, who made the sea and the dry land" (Jonah 1 v 9). In other words, the Creator of 1 v 9, who governs all the earth, is the Saviour of 4 v 2, who desires to save all nations. So the LORD's command to Jonah in 1 v 2, repeated in 3 v 2, "*Go* to the great city of Nineveh", was always about saving sinners, just as the risen Jesus was always going to use his enthronement in power for evangelism, commanding us, "*Go* and make disciples of all nations" (Matthew 28 v 19).

Chapter 4 now builds towards a final crescendo, the climactic punchline of the book in the LORD's probing question that calls to us across the centuries: "Should I not have concern for the great city of Nineveh?" (Jonah 4 v 11). His desire is not the destruction the Ninevites deserve but the mercy he wants to show. For, as Peter later explains, "He is patient with you, not wanting anyone to perish, but everyone to come to repentance" (2 Peter 3 v 9). But as we see from his response, Jonah is a long way from being godly:

> "But Jonah was greatly displeased [this literally says he considered it 'evil'—a word used repeatedly here] and became angry." (Jonah 4 v 1, NIV84)

Jonah was angry because, when God saw how the Ninevites turned from their "evil", he had compassion and did not bring upon them the "evil" he had threatened. Jonah then considered this mercy to be "evil" and became so angry he wanted to die. He actually thought God had become evil in showing mercy. He thought it was morally disgusting for the LORD to welcome these Assyrians into the blessings of Israel— and it made him apoplectic with rage.

Complaining about God's love

Now before we dismiss Jonah too quickly, it's worth remembering that these Ninevites were extremely violent, immoral and idolatrous. We easily forget that when their armies swept through the region, they brought a tsunami of violence—they skinned, skewered and beheaded captured

118

leaders, butchered captive soldiers, burned children alive, and raped, enslaved and deported their women. Asking Jonah to enjoy the salvation of Nineveh was like asking persecuted Christians in Syria today to welcome into their churches converts from ISIS who have killed and maimed their families.

Jonah finally explodes and pours out the poison of his soul to God, revealing that it wasn't fear but disgust at the LORD's extravagant mercy that drove him to flee from the LORD in the first place! Using Israel's special covenant name for God (LORD, see page 24), he protests at God extending his mercy so far beyond Israel:

> "He prayed to the LORD, 'Isn't this what I said, LORD,
> when I was still at home? That is what I tried to forestall
> by fleeing to Tarshish. I **knew** that you are a gracious and
> compassionate God, slow to anger and abounding in love, a
> God who relents from sending calamity.'"
>
> (Jonah 4 v 2, bold text mine)

Jonah quotes half of the glorious long name of the LORD revealed to Moses in Exodus 34 v 6-7 to identify exactly what he is finding so difficult about God. He ignores the second part of God's name, concerned with punishing the guilty (because he's quite happy with that), and complains about five wonderful attributes of God:

"Gracious"—God's undeserved and extraordinary generosity in providing all that we need. This is especially wonderful in giving to us, in Christ, the righteousness that we need to qualify us for heaven. Let me illustrate. A few years ago I was invited to a friend's fiftieth party, which had a James Bond film theme. All the men were expected to come in tuxedo dinner suits. The only tuxedo I could find at home was now far too small and utterly filthy. I couldn't go to the party in that! So I had to borrow a clean suit from a friend to get into the celebration. In the same way, none of us will qualify for heaven in our own lives, which are too filthy for heaven. We have to "borrow" Christ's perfect Christian life—lived for us as our King, to qualify us for the great banquet in heaven. This is "**G**od's **R**ighteousness **A**t **C**hrist's **E**xpense" (G.R.A.C.E.).

"**Compassionate**" (merciful)—the partner to God's generous grace is his patient mercy, *withholding the punishment* we deserve and suffering it himself in Christ. The moving story is told of a young boy who was deeply embarrassed by the horribly scarred hands of his older brother. The whole school laughed at those hands and the younger brother felt increasingly ashamed, until one day his mother caught him crying with frustration and explained: when he was just a toddler, the younger boy had reached up to a saucepan of boiling water on the stove and was about to pull it down onto himself, when his older brother saw what was happening and grabbed the boiling saucepan with his bare hands. Despite the agonising pain, he had taken the pan to the kitchen sink and poured the water away. Even after months of operations, his hands had been irreparably disfigured. After a long silence, the small boy whispered, "I think I like my brother's hands now, because they were scarred for me". That is something of what our older brother did for us on the cross so that we can experience God's mercy.

"**Slow to anger**"—think of the long-suffering patience of a young mother who, despite being exhausted by broken nights and frustrated by the endless crying of her baby, tenderly cares for her child. In the same way, God endures our nauseating greed and pride and selfishness with amazingly patient tolerance.

"Abounding in love"—God's love is like the never-ending torrents of water at the Niagara Falls, for ever *pardoning* our sins, *protecting* us from evil, and *providing* our daily needs.

"Who relents from sending calamity"—having planned from before the creation of the world to answer the prayers of rebels, God had kept his promise to forgive the Ninevites when they cried out to him in prayers of repentant faith—just like the father who forgave and celebrated his rebellious son when he came to his senses and came home (Luke 15).

But Jonah just can't stand how kind God is. "Now, LORD, take away my life, for it is better for me to die than to live" (Jonah 4 v 3). In other words, *I'd rather die than witness this. I don't want to be in the world with you in it, if this is how you behave.* He's just like the self-righteous older son in Jesus' parable, who ended up outside the father's banquet because he never really loved his father—he'd just religiously slaved away in the hope of earning a party with his friends. So he couldn't stomach the grace of his father in forgiving his wayward brother. Likewise, Jonah can't stand the Lord who is "God our Saviour, who wants all people to be saved and to come to a knowledge of the truth" (1 Timothy 2 v 3-4). Though Jonah himself has only just been saved from drowning, Jonah's hatred of the Assyrians has now become a hatred of God! So God asks Jonah a question he'll repeat in verse 9:

> *"But the LORD replied, 'Is it right for you to be angry?'"*
>
> *(Jonah 4 v 4)*

God is effectively asking, *Who on earth do you think you are?* God ignores Jonah's idiotic request for assisted suicide and demands that Jonah consider what right he has to feel resentful of others being blessed? What right do we have to feel annoyed if our church switches its attention from caring for us to the international café reaching immigrant workers? Or if funds are diverted from our church camp to a Bible-translation project in Mozambique? Or if we're asked to host foreign students for lunch instead of our friends? What right do we have to get annoyed by a family from a different culture noisily arriving late, or an old guy who's new to church needing to go out for a smoke during the service, or by those who struggle with English, by those who hate the drums, by a single mum getting lots of attention or being slow to take her crying baby out, or by elderly people who talk during the sermon? What right do we have to feel annoyed? Or have we forgotten that we'd be suffering in hell if not for the same grace now being shown to them?

We're not told if Jonah's disgust was primarily a self-righteous religious scorn for pagan idolaters, a racist hostility towards the violent enemies of Israel, or despair at how soft the LORD was proving to be! Most probably a toxic cocktail of all three. But he'd clearly forgotten the role of Israel as God's priesthood for introducing God to the nations (Exodus 19 v 5-6) and his own role as a prophet of God to proclaim God's word. Perhaps we too easily forget that we're saved from sin for God's evangelistic, church-planting and cross-cultural mission to all nations—so Paul writes, "He died for all, that those who live should no longer live for themselves but for him who died for them" (2 Corinthians 5 v 15).

What is quite clear is that Jonah felt no compassion for these foreigners. Although he had learned in the fish to be obedient and to preach the gospel of judgment, he had allowed his racial and cultural prejudice to strangle his love for unbelievers. And I think that many of us are much more like him than we dare admit. Many of us who faithfully proclaim the gospel of judgment have never truly embraced those who are different to ourselves, perhaps the Asians, the homosexuals or the poor who are coming to our churches in hope of salvation. So God is about to teach Jonah and us something truly wonderful…

OUR LORD IS FULL OF COMPASSION

Read Jonah 4 v 5-11

How will we ever become useful to God in his global evangelistic, church-planting and cross-cultural mission? How can we and our churches become more evangelistic? What has to change for us to become more effective at reaching the lost? Our Lord is about to tell us.

At a time when Britain and America have recently revealed some unpleasant resentment of our immigrant communities, and mission agencies report a troubling downturn in applications to serve in gospel ministry overseas, the story of Jonah challenges our neglect and fear of evangelism. Let's look into the mirror that God has provided for us in the prophet Jonah, and face some fairly ugly truths:

Jonah wanted God's grace for himself

"Jonah had gone out and sat down at a place east of the city.
There he made himself a shelter, sat in its shade and waited
to see what would happen to the city." (Jonah 4 v 5)

Can you picture Jonah? Having complained bitterly about
the LORD showing mercy towards the people of Nineveh,
he trudged off to sit on a hill on the outskirts of the city to
wait for the forty-day period that he'd proclaimed to expire.
Presumably he sat there alone, muttering angrily to himself
and seething with hatred, hoping that God would still rain
down the fires of hell on Nineveh, as he once had on Sodom
and Gomorrah. How pathetically selfish! Jonah's teaching had
just been used by God to bring a whole city to repentance—
his urban church-plant had exploded with growth into a
megachurch of 120,000. They urgently needed instruction in
the Scriptures, and he was God's trained prophet. But he was
sitting on his own feeling sorry for himself—having a tantrum.

Jonah must have known that the LORD is a cross-cultural
missionary. Back in Genesis, having scattered the nations,
who had united against him, God promised Abraham that
he would bless all nations through his kingdom (Genesis 12
v 3). In the national model of this kingdom, he redeemed
Israel from slavery to become his holy priesthood—to make
God known to all nations—and then he welcomed believing
foreigners like Rahab and Ruth into his people and into the
family ancestry of his great king David—indeed of Jesus
himself (Ruth 4; Matthew 1). The LORD promised a son to
David who would also be his own Son, to inherit and govern
all nations (2 Samuel 7). He invited rebellious global leaders

to submit to this son (Psalm 2) and to come and enjoy the legendary wisdom of this king, as the astonished queen of Sheba did when she visited Solomon (1 Kings 10). God sent prophets to warn all nations of his coming wrath (Ezekiel 1 – 24), called all nations to make pilgrimage to the mountain of the LORD (Isaiah 2) and promised his people in exile a Messiah who would be the light for all nations.

After Jonah's time, when this Christ arrived, foreign Magi came to worship him (Matthew 2). Jesus called his disciples to learn to fish for people (Matthew 4), and after dying for his elect from all nations, he rose to commission his followers to go and make disciples of them, promising to be with us to the end of the age (Matthew 28). Having ascended on high, he poured out his Spirit to empower his witnesses to take the gospel to the ends of the earth (Acts 1 – 2). He taught his apostle Peter that he does not show favouritism and that there is one Name by which all nations can be saved (Acts 10 v 34-35). He converted Paul to be his apostle to the nations. He trains us to be culturally flexible without compromising the message: to be all things to all people so that by all possible means we might save some (1 Corinthians 9).

Then, to encourage us in his global evangelism, church-planting and cross-cultural mission, he has provided the most thrilling final vision of the magnificent multicultural feast of the Lamb in heaven, where we shall celebrate our missionary Lord in a multitude that no one can count, from every nation, tribe, people and language (Revelation 7). What a festival that promises to be—making our famous Notting Hill Carnival in London seem small and dull by comparison, because the crowds will be far bigger, the diversity far greater and the joy far deeper, and because the King of all nations will be there in all his glory. It is now obvious that the Lord had always planned to exalt and delight his Son by gathering a grateful people from all nations to be united to Christ as his bride for ever, rejoicing in his sacrificial love.

But Jonah did not yet share our Lord's priorities! So God had to discipline Jonah… again! In the fish Jonah had to learn to *love God*; now he must learn to *love unbelievers*:

- Verse 6: "Then the LORD God *provided* a leafy plant and made it grow up over Jonah to give shade for his head to ease his discomfort, and Jonah was very happy about the plant"—this was probably a castor-oil plant, another experience of the generous *provision* of God.
- Verse 7: "But at dawn the next day God *provided* a worm, which chewed the plant so that it withered"—this *provision* of a worm was to kill the plant so as to give God the opportunity to lovingly disciple Jonah.
- Verse 8: "When the sun rose, God *provided* a scorching east wind, and the sun blazed on Jonah's head so that he grew faint. He wanted to die, and said, 'It would be better for me to die than to live'"—God *provided* this scorching wind to "turn up the heat" in his evangelism training. Jonah was again afflicted with a seriously self-pitying death wish. So the LORD asks him the same question again…
- Verse 9: "Is it right for you to be angry about the plant?"—the implication being, it isn't!
- Verse 10: "But the LORD said, 'You have been concerned about this plant, though you did not

tend it or make it grow. It sprang up overnight and died overnight'"—*You seem more concerned about this single bush that you've enjoyed for one day than for a whole city of people whose eternity is at stake!* This is like Christians who are more concerned for their garden than for their neighbours—putting more effort into their lawn than into their friendship with the African family next door. How can we be so selfish?

- Verse 11: "The great city of Nineveh, in which there are more than a hundred and twenty thousand people who cannot tell their right hand from their left—and also many animals"—*Jonah, can't you see that this city of people (and even the animals that I've created), are more deserving of your concern than the shelter over your head?* This is as pitiful as people who spend more time and money on the interior of their house than on gospel work. How can we be so selfish?

And now we discover the reason that Jonah wants God's grace for himself…

Jonah lacked God's concern for the lost

The LORD said in verse 11:

> *"Should I not have concern for the great city of Nineveh?"*

Now the thoughtful Bible student might again wonder about God showing such concern, because of his "*impassibility*". This is his freedom from being subject to pain or emotion caused by others; for the supreme being cannot be the victim of

others, and God is completely self-sufficient (in his "aseity")—
he doesn't need anything. God doesn't save people because he
needs company, and he doesn't use us in evangelism because
he needs help. He graciously invites us to share in his mission
but if we won't, he'll use someone else; because we're not the
Saviour of the world—he is. And we can sleep at night trusting
God to save all his chosen people! But he does command us
to make disciples of all nations *in order to share his compassion
for the lost* and to test and purify our obedience by giving us
opportunities to please him, because he wants to reward us
in eternity for the sacrificial evangelism that God is all about.

God certainly cannot suffer damage to his own being or
character; but gloriously, from eternity past he has volunteered
to accept the pain and grief of loving sinners like us. God
the Son volunteered to become human to suffer for us on
the cross, and God the Father volunteered for the grief of
watching his only Son suffer. Never as our victim—always
freely volunteering to give himself to us in extraordinary,
compassionate love.

So in the Gospels we read of Jesus evangelising, and "when
he saw the crowds, he had compassion on them, because they
were harassed and helpless, like sheep without a shepherd"
(Matthew 9 v 36). This particular word, "*compassion*", is used
only in the Gospels, always of Christ, and always of how he
regarded crowds of people. The word means "entrails" and
describes his *gut-wrenching tenderness* towards people who
he can see are "harassed and helpless" (literally "flayed" and
"crushed", or as we might say, "stressed and burdened"), like
"sheep without a shepherd", meaning lost without him. (For
example, Matthew 14 v 14: "When Jesus landed and saw

a large crowd, he had compassion on them…"; Matthew 15 v 32: "Jesus called his disciples to him and said, "I have compassion for these people"; and Matthew 20 v 34: "Jesus had compassion on them".)

When Jesus sees a rowdy football crowd, he doesn't condemn them as an angry mob but feels *gut-wrenching compassion* for them as people who desperately need him. When Jesus looks at commuters pouring in and out of the city to work, he doesn't despise them as selfish materialists but feels a *gut-wrenching tenderness* for people who desperately need him. When he sees a political rally protesting in front of Parliament or a gay pride march, or retired middle classes relaxing in luxury on a cruise ship, or young people swarming among the shops in search of bargains, he doesn't despise them as we commonly do. Jesus feels a *gut-wrenching tenderness* for people who desperately need him.

But Jonah didn't feel the way Jesus feels at all. The poet Thomas Carlyle wrote these lines to describe Jonah's selfish heart:

> *"And Jonah stalked*
> *to his shaded seat*
> *and waited for God*
> *to come around*
> *to his way of thinking.*
>
> *And God is still waiting for a host of Jonahs*
> *in their comfortable houses*
> *to come around*
> *to his way of loving."*

The reason Jonah didn't want to go to Nineveh was that he just didn't love those immoral foreigners. And I now realise that the primary reason we struggle to evangelise our communities is not that they are more hostile than those of another culture or a previous generation, but that we just don't love them enough. Most of us don't need more training—we need to share Christ's gut-wrenching compassion towards people who are different from us.

Compassion for people will motivate us to get involved in evangelism

In Matthew 9 v 37, Jesus identified two features of our age: first, "the harvest is plentiful". There are plenty of opportunities because the culture is not too hard (we might say one cemetery is only as dead as another), so it depends how we see our neighbourhood or office. The story is told of a shoe-company salesman sent to West Africa to sell shoes. After six months he sent the following miserable report back to head office: "Situation hopeless—no one wears any shoes here—bring me home immediately!" A second salesman was then sent out to the same place, and after six months sent a completely different report: "Situation fantastic—no one wears any shoes here—send all the shoes you can find!" The fact that we are surrounded by unbelievers in Western cities is not a cause for self-pitying despair but for exciting, prayerful missionary activity. As in other Western cities, more than 90% of Londoners claim no saving faith in Christ. So what a wonderful place for a Christian to live, on the mission-field. When we go to our offices or building sites or children's playgrounds, we are surrounded by evangelistic opportunities.

Here is a Hindu, two atheists, a Muslim, a Roman Catholic and a Satanist—all in need of a Saviour. Almost any casual conversation is an opportunity for evangelism if we look for it.

But the second feature of our times that Jesus observed was this: "the workers are few". Notice that Jesus didn't say the clergy are too few! We don't just need more clergy; we need people of every kind with a little gut-wrenching compassion in their hearts. We must pray for more people committed to evangelism; pray for more churches committed to being lifeboats with crew dedicated to reaching those who are drowning in sin, rather than cruise ships half-full of passengers dedicated to their own comfort; and pray for more pastors, preachers, planters, pioneers, patrons and gospel workers of every kind.

Compassion for people will motivate us to get involved in church-planting

There's no command in the Bible to plant churches, but ever since the apostle Paul, evangelism has resulted in churches being planted, and planting churches has proved the single most effective way of evangelising a community and city. Our own goal in London is to plant and strengthen 60 diverse reformed evangelical churches across London by 2025, through both planting and revitalisation, and 360 in the long term, for the salvation of many to the glory of God. We may well fail, but we're going to give it a go and not die wondering. What could you and your church plan to do towards planting and revitalising churches to reach the lost?

Compassion for people will motivate us to get involved in cross-cultural mission

In London our network of churches is currently launching our very modest "Open Hand" shared minimal commitment to extend our cross-cultural mission. We've called it "Open Hand" to illustrate our desire to give generously of ourselves and our resources, to *extend a hand of friendship* in gospel ministry to God's people everywhere, and to resist the temptation to think of international mission as the "sore thumb" that taxes our church-planting, and instead *give our whole hand to being cross-cultural* in everything we do.

There are five themes that "Open Hand" will focus upon to build upon what many churches are already doing, and we have asked five respected evangelical mission agencies with whom we already partner to help train us in one theme each. It now seems obvious that churches in cities like London need to seek help in cross-cultural mission from global mission agencies, because such mission agencies know what they're doing. Our five themes are:

a. *Welcome*—we've asked for help to become churches that are more welcoming to people from different cultures, especially by helping our churches to provide excellent international cafes.

b. *Host*—we've asked for help to become churches that are able to reach local ethnic communities, especially by securing and training a cross-cultural worker for each of our churches.

c. *Plant*—we've asked for help to plant churches in different cultural communities in London—and especially by working with us to train cross-cultural pioneers.

d. *Send*—we have asked for help to recruit and deploy workers for a variety of missions fields—and especially by developing a range of short term mission placements for younger people exploring possibilities.

e. *Pray*—we've asked for help to become churches who pray, especially for all who are persecuted for our faith, and especially our brothers and sisters in the Arab world during the month of Ramadan.

This is hardly rocket science, but we're trying to make a start. Perhaps you can go much further.

Here is Hudson Taylor's account of the decisive moment when his Christ-like compassion finally conquered his anxieties, and he surrendered himself to go to China, where God used him to grow the China Inland Mission, which contributed so signally to what is now reckoned to be more than 100 million believers in China.

> *"On Sunday, June 25th 1865, unable to bear the sight of a congregation of a thousand or more Christian people rejoicing in their own security, while millions were perishing for lack of knowledge, I wandered out on the sands alone, in great spiritual agony; and there the Lord conquered my unbelief, and I surrendered myself for this service. I told him that all the responsibility as to issues and consequences must rest with him, that as his servant, it was mine to obey and*

follow him—his to direct, to care for, and to guide me and those who might labour with me."

> Taylor, J. H. (n.d.). A Retrospect (Third Edition,
> p 119–120). Toronto: China Inland Mission

This is the gut-wrenching compassion that we find in our Lord in Jonah, in Jesus in the Gospels, and in the Holy Spirit who is now empowering global evangelism, church-planting and cross-cultural mission. Let us pray for such compassion right now... for the book of Jonah is not really about Jonah the reluctant evangelist at all. It's about our Lord the sovereign, gracious, merciful and compassionate Evangelist, who told Jonah, "Go..." and in Jesus tells *us, "Go and make disciples of all nations".*

APPENDIX 1: THE GOSPEL

Many Christians assume that the gospel is everything good about being Christian, but that's not what the Bible says. Since the gospel is "the power of God that brings salvation" (Romans 1 v 16), we need to know what the gospel really is so that we can be saved and then proclaim it to our families, friends and colleagues so they can be saved too.

The word "gospel" just means "good news". It was used in the Roman Empire of New Testament times for momentous public announcements such as the birth of an emperor or a victory in battle. The "gospel of God" is his sensational announcement to his world (Romans 1 v 1-17), progressively revealed throughout the Bible.

In the Old Testament God's gospel promised a kingdom and a King

The gospel was first announced in God's promise to Abraham of a land, a nation and blessing: *a kingdom* bringing blessing to all nations (read Genesis 12 v 1-3—called "the gospel" in Galatians 3 v 8). The history of Israel then provides an earthly picture of a future heavenly kingdom through which wonderful eternal blessings will come.

God announced his gospel again in Isaiah's repeated promises of *a King* for his kingdom (read Isaiah 40 v 9-11; 52 v 7-10; 61 v 1-2). They announce that the Lord himself will come like a shepherd gathering his lambs. He will reign over all and will reveal his salvation to all nations. And he will liberate his people from captivity far from God and gather them into his kingdom. Astonishingly, this mighty deliverer would be the Lord's suffering servant, accepting the punishment for our sin in his death, and then rising to life to "justify" (qualify) many for heaven (Isaiah 53 v 4-6, 11-12).

In the history of Israel, God provided many judges, prophets, priests, kings and governors to provide us with pictures and prophecies to give us descriptions of this wonderful Saviour and King. As with a jigsaw puzzle, you start with the corners and edge pieces to form an outline, but it's only when the final pieces are placed in the middle that the picture is complete and makes sense. So the promises of the Old Testament provided an outline of the coming King, but it wasn't then clear how God's King could possibly bring sinners from all nations into his heavenly kingdom.

But then there was silence for centuries… until the explosive moment when a tradesman's son emerged onto the public stage, "proclaiming the good news [gospel] of God. 'The time has come,' he said. 'The kingdom of God has come near. Repent and believe the good news [gospel]!" (Mark 1 v 14-15)

In the New Testament God's gospel announces that Jesus is our Lord and Saviour

The mystery of the gospel becomes crystal clear in the New Testament when Jesus is unveiled as the long-awaited King, saving us into his kingdom. There are many versions of God's gospel because it's about a person, not a formula. But two glorious themes emerge in them all: *Jesus is our Lord* (who he is) and *Jesus is our Saviour* (what he's done). Both are stunningly good news for us today.

Jesus is our Lord

In Romans 1 v 1-4, Paul explains the gospel of God to show why all nations need to hear it. He says it's "regarding his Son". If we're not talking about Jesus, we're not talking about the gospel. When we talk about our experience, our church, our sin, or even God the Father and God the Holy Spirit, we are speaking of great biblical truths but not about the gospel that saves people. Paul often summarises God's gospel regarding his Son with the phrase, *"Jesus Christ our Lord"* (Romans 1 v 4; Colossians 2 v 6; 2 Corinthians 4 v 5). Obviously, this isn't his first name, middle name and surname.

- *"Jesus"* means the crucified Galilean of history.
- *"Christ"* means the promised Saviour King of the Old Testament.
- *"Lord"* means the divine and risen Ruler of all.

God's gospel tells us how amazing Jesus is: *Jesus is Christ our Lord.* It then tells us what he's done…

Jesus is our Saviour

God's gospel celebrates Christ's four primary achievements:

Christ came as our King (Mark 1 v 14-15)—Mark's Gospel is entitled "The good news [gospel] about Jesus the Messiah"

(Mark 1 v 1). Mark then announces, "Jesus went into Galilee, proclaiming the good news [gospel] of God ... 'The kingdom of God has come near!'" (Mark 1 v 14-15). Jesus is the long-awaited King, rescuing people into his heavenly kingdom. He demonstrated the fabulous benefits of life under his rule with his merciful forgiveness, his wise teaching and his compassionate miracles. Though the Gospels and epistles concentrate on Christ's death and resurrection, we should remember that this is how our King brings us into his kingdom. Indeed, this message is how his kingdom grows in the world today, as people surrender to his rule and become citizens of his coming new-creation kingdom.

Christ died for our sins (1 Corinthians 15 v 1-4)—Paul reminds the Corinthians of God's saving gospel: "Christ died for our sins according to the Scriptures". Christ's death was incredibly special because he died (voluntarily and not as a victim) for our sins (as our loving self-sacrificial substitute). His death is special because he died "according to the Scriptures"—to satisfy the justice of God as our "Passover sacrifice", our "atonement sacrifice" and our "suffering-servant sacrifice". Paul reminds us that despite the claims of many that Jesus merely swooned, his death is undeniable because he was buried by his friends.

Christ rose to rule (1 Corinthians 15 v 4-7)—Paul continues, "He was raised on the third day according to the Scriptures". The New Testament triumphantly proclaims that, as promised by the Old Testament and by himself, Jesus was raised to life and enthroned in heaven. He is now King over us all because he completely paid for all our sins—and we are completely qualified for heaven in him. Paul reminds us that his resurrection is also undeniable because "he appeared" to so many people.

Christ will return to judge (Romans 2 v 16)—many Christians are unaware that Scripture explicitly says that judgment is part of the gospel. For example, Paul describes "the day when *God will judge men's secrets through Jesus Christ*" as "my gospel" (Romans 2 v 16; see also Revelation 14 v 6). Jesus consistently taught that his judgment will begin an eternity of extravagant blessing in his renewed creation for all his repentant followers, but an eternity of torment in hell for his unrepentant enemies.

The spectacular benefit of God's gospel is life in his heavenly kingdom

We also find God's gospel described as the gospel of *peace, hope, life, righteousness and grace*. This is not to say that if we talk about peace or justice, we are proclaiming the gospel. Rather, these words describe the beautiful benefits of the gospel for all who believe it. So when we turn to Jesus, we begin to experience the reassuring comfort of *peace* with God even amid tragedy and pain, the uplifting encouragement of our certain *hope* of being with him, the deep satisfaction of abundant *life* in personal relationship with him, and the joy of Christ's *righteousness* counted as ours and growing within us. By faith in the gospel, we begin to taste the sweet generosity of God's *grace*. And one day, when Jesus returns, we'll know all these joys perfectly in heaven. These benefits of the gospel are actually life in the kingdom of God: the blessing originally promised to Abraham.